All Through the Woods

QUILTED PROJECTS FROM THE NORTH COUNTRY

CORI DERKSEN & MYRA HARDER

Martingale™
& COMPANY

DEDICATION

Cori

A very special thank you to my husband and daughter:

To Randy for your encouragement and support, for never shaking your head when I'm starting another project or power quilting to get one done, for going out at 9 o'clock in the evening to look for the perfect branch to hang a project from, and for truly appreciating the quilts that I have made.

To my two-year-old daughter, Kierra, who has two-hour afternoon naps so that Mommy can work on projects like this book without interruption. We have both been known to have disagreements on whose turn it should be to sit in my office chair or who should use the computer first! Kierra, I hope that someday you, too, will enjoy the art of quilting.

Thank you to my family and friends for encouraging me in my hobby and business endeavors!

Myra

To the two outdoorsmen of my life: my husband, Mark, and our son, Samson.

Mark has a huge love for the outdoors, and Sam is ready to be his shadow and follow in his father's ways as soon as he can. Thank you, Mark, for being patient and supportive, even when my ideas flood into every part of the house. And thank you most of all for being so outwardly proud that I can sew, yet inwardly wonder why I can't mend pants.

ACKNOWLEDGMENTS

Our sincere thanks and appreciation go to:

Family and friends, for sharing in our enthusiasm for our hobby;

Betty Klassen, who is Myra's mom, our boss, our best critic, and our greatest fan;

Meg Suderman and Lydia Zacharias, our coworkers, who never question our judgment and skillfully appliqué and quilt many of our pieces;

Marlene Lindal, our photographer, who never complained while trudging through snowbanks on a *very* cold winter's day to take our picture; and

Martingale & Company—it has been a pleasure working with you!

CREDITS

President . . . . Nancy J. Martin
CEO . . . . Daniel J. Martin
Publisher . . . . Jane Hamada
Editorial Director . . . . Mary V. Green
Editorial Project Manager . . . . Tina Cook
Technical Editor . . . . Dawn Anderson
Copy Editor . . . . Liz McGehee
Design and Production Manager . . . . Stan Green
Illustrator . . . . Laurel Strand
Cover Designer . . . . Stan Green
Text Designer . . . . Jennifer LaRock Shontz
Photographer . . . . Brent Kane

That Patchwork Place® is an imprint of Martingale & Company™.

All through the Woods: Quilted Projects from the North Country
© 2001 by Cori Derksen and Myra Harder

Martingale & Company
20205 144th Avenue NE
Woodinville, WA 98072-8478 USA
www.martingale-pub.com

Printed in Hong Kong
06 05 04 03 02 01   8 7 6 5 4 3 2 1

MISSION STATEMENT

We are dedicated to providing quality products and service by working together to inspire creativity and to enrich the lives we touch.

Library of Congress Cataloging-in-Publication Data

Derksen, Cori
  All through the woods : quilted projects from the
  North Country / Cori Derksen & Myra Harder.
    p. cm.
  ISBN 1-56477-407-4
    1. Patchwork–Patterns. 2. Appliqué–Patterns. 3. Quilting.
  4. Forests in art. 5. Wilderness areas in art. I. Harder, Myra.
  II. Title.

TT835 .D46297 2001
746.46'041—dc21   2001045003

Contents

Introduction

The idea for *All through the Woods* came from the mere sketch of a moose! It didn't take long before we had a whole collection of wilderness projects. Our goal in writing this book was to create uncomplicated projects suited for both the beginner and the experienced quilter. The beginner can tackle these projects with confidence and learn all the basic skills that quilting requires, such as simple appliqué, basic piecing, working with color, and experi-menting with different quilting styles. The experienced quilter will enjoy taking a break from other quilting endeavors to complete these fast and fun projects at a relaxed pace.

Some of our projects have a touch of whimsy while others offer a true impression—all of which we hope you will enjoy! The projects in this book are a reflection of our personal style. What better way to bring the outdoors in to enjoy!

Fabric Choices

We love cottons! We find cotton to be the least frustrating fabric to work with, and the final projects are quite rewarding. Besides, there are so many beautiful cotton prints and plaids available that it is hard not to be drawn to them. Also, historically, it has been proven that cotton quilts last for many genera-tions. So if you do it right the first time, many people will be able to enjoy your work for years to come. We used a lot of plaids in these projects; we feel they add to the outdoors feeling. Do not be afraid of using plaids and prints. Be creative with your fabric choices, for this adds character to your quilts. These projects are a great way to use scraps from your own fabric stash.

Paper-Piecing Instructions

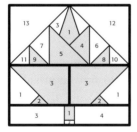 The only paper piecing in this book is found in the flag block in "North of the Forty-Nine" on page 9. Patterns are given for both the Canadian and American flags.

1. Transfer the pattern for either the Canadian or American flag (pages 46–47) onto your desired foundation paper. Cut out the block along the dark solid line that runs around the pattern's outer edges. Cut the multiple-unit block (Canadian flag) apart along each dark solid line. Keep in mind that the pattern is the finished size of the block, so the fabric pieces need to extend at least ¼" beyond the paper foundation to act as your seam allowance.

Single-unit block

Multiple-unit block

2. Set your sewing machine's stitch length for 15 to 18 stitches per inch. Insert a 90/14 needle into the machine. If the paper tears away as you sew, decrease the number of stitches per inch; if the stitches loosen up as you pull the paper foundation away, increase the number of stitches per inch. It isn't necessary to backstitch because the closeness of the stitches keeps the pieces from pulling apart.

3. Place each unit of the pattern in front of you with the marked side facing up. This will be referred to as the pattern right side. The unmarked side will be referred to as the wrong side.

4. For each unit, cut a piece of fabric for the part marked 1. Be sure it is at least ¼" larger all the way around than the size of the part it will cover. Do not attempt to cut the fabric to size. Just be sure the fabric amply covers the part; the excess will be trimmed away later.

5. Hold the unit up to a light with the marked side (right side) facing you. Place the wrong side of fabric piece 1 on the wrong side of the pattern so the fabric covers part 1. Temporarily pin the piece in place. When you hold the block up to the light, the fabric should cover part 1.

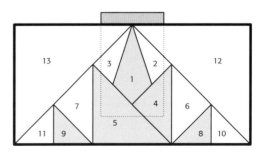

6. Cut a piece of fabric at least ½" larger all the way around than part 2.

7. Hold the unit up to a light with the right side of the pattern facing you. Place fabric piece 2 over fabric piece 1, right sides together, with at least ¼" of fabric extending over the line that separates parts 1 and 2.

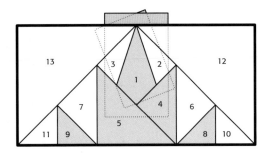

8. Working on the right side of the pattern, sew along the thin black line that separates parts 1 and 2.

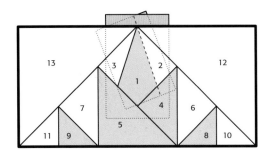

9. Fold back piece 2 along the seam line. Hold the unit up to the light. Be sure that parts 1 and 2 are covered and that the fabric piece for each part extends at least ¼" on all sides.

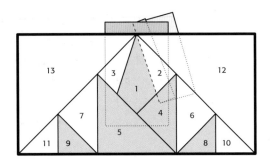

10. Working on the pattern wrong side, fold piece 2 back down so the wrong side of the fabric is face up. Trim the seam allowance between parts 1 and 2 to ¼". If the excess fabric isn't trimmed away, it can eventually build up and make quilting more difficult later.

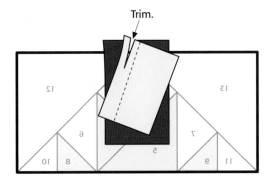

11. Fold piece 2 open. Finger-press or use a wooden pressing tool to press the seam allowance flat.

12. Continue adding fabric pieces, in numerical order, in the same manner for the remaining parts.

13. When you have added all of the fabric pieces to each block or unit, lightly press each block or unit and trim the outer seam allowances to ¼".

14. If you are piecing a multiple-unit block, stitch the units together so they are a mirror image of the pattern. Remember, the finished block is a mirror image of the pattern. Lightly press the block.

15. Remove the paper foundation.

Helpful Hints for Paper Piecing

- Keep all threads trimmed short. They love to get caught in your machine and jam things up.
- Always press the completed units before joining them into blocks.

Appliqué Instructions

There are several ways of using freezer paper for appliqué. The method we prefer is to place the freezer paper on the right side of the fabric, turn the seam allowances under, and stitch down the appliqué. Every new technique takes a little time to get used to, but we feel that once you have practiced this technique a few times, you will find it as simple and fast as we do. Follow these simple step-by-step instructions.

1. Use a fine-line pencil to trace the appliqué patterns onto the dull side of a piece of freezer paper. Note that some of the pattern pieces are too large to fit on one page. You will need to join the individual pieces to make your complete patterns.

2. Cut out each piece along the traced line. Do not leave any seam allowances around the pieces.

3. Place the freezer-paper piece on the right side of the appropriate fabric, shiny side down. Leave approximately ½" between pieces. Press the pieces in place with a hot iron.

4. Cut out each appliqué, leaving a ¼" seam allowance around the freezer-paper piece.

Freezer paper

5. Place the appliqué in the appropriate position on the background fabric. If needed, pin the appliqué in place, pinning through the middle of the piece so the edges are easier to reach, and appliqué under.

6. Turn a portion of the seam allowance under until it is even with the edge of the freezer paper. Using thread that is close in color to the appliqué, tie a knot at the end of the thread and secure it in the seam allowance. Taking stitches that are about ⅛" long, insert the needle into the background fabric underneath the appliqué piece. Come up through the background fabric, just catching the edge of the appliqué. Continue to repeat this process until your piece is completely stitched into place.

7. Remove the freezer paper.

Helpful Hints for Appliquéing Curved Pieces

- On inside curves, clip *slightly* into the seam allowance (do not clip the entire width of the seam allowance); this will allow the fabric to spread and lie flat.
- On outside curves, do not clip seam allowances.

Adding Details

You can have fun with these projects and incorporate your own pieces of charm into them. We have used buttons for animal eyes, the backs of the pillows, and the tabs on the wall hangings. Use embroidery, too, to add details where appropriate. We used machine stitching to add the fishing hook on "Salmon Wall Hanging" (page 38) and for the zipper of the tent in "Black Bear Pillow" (page 30).

We like to hang the smaller wall hangings on unique twigs. Consider displaying "Beaver Wall Hanging" (page 36) on a twig that came from a beaver dam and hanging "Salmon Wall Hanging" (page 38) on a homemade fishing rod. Little accents like these can add a lot of interest to the finished product.

Machine stitching was used to mimic the zippered opening on the front of the tent.

A shank button adds a dimensional eye to the loon.

The handmade fishing rod was made using a twig, some cording, and a lure. The tabs, secured in place with coordinating buttons along the top of the quilt, are used to hang the quilt from the fishing rod.

Embroidery Stitches

Satin Stitch

Bring the needle up at 1, down at 2, making parallel stitches. Repeat to fill the desired area.

Stem Stitch

Bring the needle up at 1, down at 2, and up at 3, keeping the thread to the left of the needle.

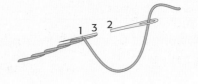

North of the Forty-Nine

North of the Forty-Nine by Myra Harder, Betty Klassen, Meg Suderman, and Lydia Zacharias, 2000, Winkler, Manitoba, 70" x 88".
This quilt includes all of the images we associate with Canada. The name of the project comes from the fact that central and western Canada begin at the forty-ninth parallel.

Plus binding of 3½" around for twin (handwritten note)

MATERIALS FOR WALL HANGING (70" X 88"): 42"-WIDE FABRIC

6 yds. total scraps or:

- *2* 1 yd. dark blue for sky
- *2* 1 yd. dark blue check for sky and flying geese
- *1½* ¾ yd. speckled medium blue for sky
- *1¼* ⅝ yd. green small check for background and cattail leaves
- *2* 1 yd. tan-and-green check for background
- *1* ½ yd. salmon check for background and salmon
- *1½* ¾ yd. medium blue check for sky
- *1¼* ⅝ yd. burnt red for background, cabin roof, and Canadian flag block (optional) *Am flag*
- *2* 1 fat quarter khaki green for background and cattail flowers
- *1* ½ yd. green large check for background *(10)*
- *2* 1 fat quarter green thin stripe for background and salmon fins
- *2* 1 fat quarter yellow for moon and star points
- *1 fat* 4" x 20" rectangle of medium red for star centers
- *½ yd* ¼ yd. dark brown for tree trunks
- *5½ yards* 5 fat quarters assorted greens for trees, cattail leaves, backgrounds, and Cabin block
- *2* 1 fat quarter black solid for large bear, bear cub, Bear Paw blocks, beaver tail, loon head, moose eyes, and ducklings
- *½* ¼ yd. medium brown for moose head and hooves, tree trunks, and cattail flowers
- *1 fat* 9" x 20" rectangle of dark brown check for moose body
- *¼ yd* 1/8 yd. tan print for snowcaps and moose antlers
- *½ yd* 1 fat quarter black print for loon and Bear Paw blocks *(20)*
- *1 yd* ½ yd. dark burnt red for mountain
- *1 fat* 6" x 11" rectangle of red for canoe
- 1 fat quarter cream for Canadian flag block (optional) and beaver tooth
- *1 fat quarter* 5" x 11" rectangle of red for American flag block (optional)
- *1 fat* 5" x 11" rectangle of white for American flag block (optional)
- *1 fat* 4" x 6" rectangle of blue star print for American flag block (optional)
- 3½" x 6½" rectangle of desired fabric for American flag block (optional)
- *1 fat* 2" x 2" square of black stripe for loon neck
- *1 fat* 8" x 10" rectangle of dark brown print for beaver body, paw, and foot
- *11 yds* 5½ yds. fabric for backing

74" x 92" piece of batting

1½ ¾ yd. fabric for binding

Sandy green embroidery floss DMC #3046

- *6* 3 tan buttons, ½" diameter, for salmon eyes
- *1* 1 black button, ⅜" diameter, for beaver eye
- *1* 1 red button, 5/16" diameter, for loon eye

MATERIALS FOR QUEEN-SIZE QUILT (88" X 106")

Materials as listed for wall hanging, except for binding, batting, and backing

⅞ yd. fabric for inner border

1⅞ yds. fabric for outer border

8 yds. fabric for backing

92" x 110" piece of batting

⅞ yd. fabric for binding

CUTTING

Note: All measurements include ¼"-wide seam allowances. Some appliqué pieces are cut from the same fabrics as the backgrounds; the appliqué pieces should be cut after the background pieces. Before cutting the pieces listed below from the assorted green fabrics, determine which of the greens will be used for tree #1, tree #2, tree #3, tree #4, and tree #5.

(1) **From the dark blue, cut:**

- 6 squares, 2⅞" x 2⅞"; cut squares once diagonally to make 12 triangles for sky (4 for Section 1 and 8 for Section 2)
- 12 squares, 2½" x 2½", for sky (4 for Section 1 and 8 for Section 2)
- 1 square, 6½" x 6½", for sky in Section 2
- 1 rectangle, 4½" x 12½", for sky in Section 2
- 1 rectangle, 16½" x 20½", for sky in Section 3
- 1 rectangle, 6½" x 14½", for sky in Section 3
- 1 rectangle, 6½" x 24½", for sky in Section 4
- 1 strip, 1½" x 16½", for sky in Section 5
- 1 strip, 2½" x 16½", for sky in Section 5

(2) **From the dark blue check, cut:**

- 1 rectangle, 8½" x 14½", for sky in Section 1
- 1 rectangle, 2½" x 6½", for sky in Section 1
- 1 strip, 4½" x 28½", for sky in Section 2
- 1 square, 6½" x 6½", for sky in Section 2
- 1 rectangle, 6½" x 10½", for sky in Section 2
- 4 squares, 2⅞" x 2⅞"; cut squares once diagonally to make 8 triangles for sky (4 for Section 2 and 4 for Section 3)

8 squares, 2½" x 2½", for sky (4 for Section 2 and 4 for Section 3)

4 squares, 4⅞" x 4⅞"; cut squares once diagonally to make 8 triangles for flying geese in Section 3

1 strip, 4½" x 24½", for sky in Section 4

2 rectangles, 3½" x 8½", for sky in Section 9

1 rectangle, 6½" x 16½", for sky in for Section 12

1 rectangle, 6½" x 13½", for sky in Section 13

3 From the speckled medium blue, cut:

1 rectangle, 10½" x 16½", for sky in Section 2

1 strip, 4½" x 20½", for sky in Section 3

1 rectangle, 4½" x 8½", for sky in Section 3

1 strip, 12½" x 30½", for sky in Section 8

4 From the green small check, cut:

2 squares, 6½" x 6½"; cut squares once diagonally to make 4 triangles for background in Section 3

1 rectangle, 4½" x 26½", for background in Section 8

1 rectangle, 8½" x 27½", for background in Section 10

1 strip, 2½" x 12½", for background in Section 12

1 rectangle, 4½" x 13½", for background in Section 13

5 From the tan-and-green check, cut:

1 rectangle, 11½" x 18½", for background in Section 4

2 rectangles, 8½" x 13½", for background in Section 4

1 rectangle, 8½" x 14½", for background in Section 5

2 rectangles, 4" x 10½", for background in Section 5

6 From the salmon check, cut:

1 rectangle, 10½" x 24½", for background in Section 5

1 square, 10½" x 10½", for background in Section 9

2 rectangles, 5" x 6½", for background in Section 9

7 From the medium blue check, cut:

1 rectangle, 4½" x 16½", for sky in Section 5

1 rectangle, 8½" x 16½", for sky in Section 8

1 rectangle, 12½" x 16½", for sky in Section 9

1 rectangle, 8½" x 12½", for sky in Section 11

1 rectangle, 4½" x 12½", for sky in Section 11

1 rectangle, 4½" x 10½", for sky in Section 12

8 From the burnt red, cut:

1 square, 8½" x 8½", for background in Section 5

---

1 square, 2½" x 2½", for background in Section 6

2 squares, 2⅞" x 2⅞"; cut squares once diagonally to make 4 triangles for background in Section 6

1 rectangle, 4½" x 10½", for background in Section 7

4 squares, 4⅞" x 4⅞"; cut squares once diagonally to make 8 triangles for background (2 for Section 8 and 6 for Section 9)

2 rectangles, 3½" x 6½", for Section 12 if making the Canadian flag block

1 rectangle, 9½" x 16½", for background in Section 13

9 From the khaki green, cut:

1 rectangle, 8½" x 10½", for background in Section 6

2 squares, 6½" x 6½"; cut squares once diagonally to make 4 triangles for background (1 for Section 8 and 3 for Section 9)

1 square, 4½" x 4½", for background in Section 11

1 rectangle, 4½" x 13½", for background in Section 11

10 From the green large check, cut:

1 strip, 2½" x 10½", for background in Section 6

1 rectangle, 8½" x 10½", for background in Section 6

1 square, 2⅜" x 2⅜"; cut square once diagonally to make 2 triangles for background in Section 6

4 squares, 2⅞" x 2⅞"; cut squares once diagonally to make 8 triangles for background in Section 7

2 squares, 2½" x 2½", for background in Section 7

1 square, 6½" x 6½", for background in Section 7

1 rectangle, 4½" x 12½", for background in Section 8

2 rectangles, 2½" x 4½", for background in Section 9

1 rectangle, 4½" x 8½", for background in Section 9

1 rectangle, 4½" x 18½", for background in Section 13

11 From the green thin stripe, cut:

1 rectangle, 8½" x 13½", for background in Section 10

1 square, 4½" x 4½", for background in Section 11

1 rectangle, 8½" x 14½", for background in Section 12

1 rectangle, 4½" x 6½", for background in Section 12

13 From the medium brown, cut:

1 strip, 1½" x 16½", for tree trunk in Section 5

1 strip, 1½" x 10½", for tree trunk in Section 5

1 strip, 1½" x 6½", for tree trunk in Section 9

14 From the dark brown, cut:

1 strip, 2½" x 13½", for tree trunk in Section 4

1 strip, 2½" x 24½", for tree trunk in Section 5

1 rectangle, 2½" x 3½", for tree trunk in Section 6
1 rectangle, 2½" x 5½", for tree trunk in Section 6
1 square, 2⅜" x 2⅜"; cut square once diagonally to make 2 triangles for tree trunk in Section 6
1 rectangle, 2½" x 8½", for tree trunk in Section 10

From the same green as tree #1, cut:
1 rectangle, 4½" x 13½", for background in Section 11

From the same green as tree #2, cut:
1 rectangle, 2½" x 4½", for Cabin block in Section 9

From the same green as tree #3, cut:
1 rectangle, 2½" x 6½", for background in Section 6
1 rectangle, 4½" x 8½", for background in Section 6
1 rectangle, 4½" x 6½", for background in Section 7
2 rectangles, 2½" x 6½", for background in Section 9
1 rectangle, 5½" x 8½", for background in Section 12

From the same green as tree #4, cut:
1 square, 6½" x 6½", for background in Section 7
1 rectangle, 7½" x 8½", for background in Section 12

From the same green as tree #5, cut:
1 rectangle, 4½" x 18½", for background in Section 7
1 rectangle, 4½" x 13½", for background in Section 11
1 square, 4½" x 4½", for background in Section 11
1 strip, 2½" x 9½", for background in Section 13

From the black solid, cut:
3 squares, 4½" x 4½", for Bear Paw blocks (1 for Section 6 and 2 for Section 7)

From the black print, cut:
6 squares, 2⅞" x 2⅞"; cut squares once diagonally to make 12 triangles for Bear Paw blocks (4 for Section 6 and 8 for Section 7)

From the yellow, cut:
10 squares, 2⅞" x 2⅞"; cut squares once diagonally to make 20 triangles for star points (4 for Section 1, 12 for Section 2, and 4 for Section 3)

From the medium red, cut:
5 squares, 2½" x 2½", for star centers (1 for Section 1, 3 for Section 2, and 1 for Section 3)

SECTION 1
Making the Friendship Star Block

1. Join a dark blue triangle and a yellow triangle to make a half-square-triangle unit. Repeat to make 4 half-square-triangle units.

Make 4.

2. Join a 2½" dark blue square to each side of a half-square-triangle unit as shown to make Row 1.

Row 1

3. Join a half-square-triangle unit to each side of a medium red square as shown to make Row 2.

Row 2

4. Join a 2½" dark blue square to each side of a half-square-triangle unit as shown to make Row 3.

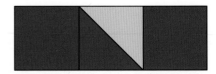

Row 3

5. Sew Rows 1–3 together to make a Friendship Star block.

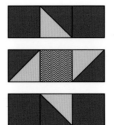

Make 1.

Assembling Section 1

1. Join the 2½" x 6½" dark blue-check rectangle to the left edge of the Friendship Star block.

2. Join the 8½" x 14½" dark blue-check rectangle to the top of the pieced Friendship Star block to complete Section 1.

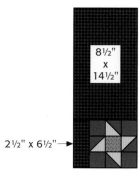

Section 1

SECTION 2

1. Follow steps 1–5 in "Making the Friendship Star Block" on page 12 to assemble 2 Friendship Star blocks for Section 2. Make a third block, substituting dark blue check for the dark blue fabric.

2. Join a dark blue Friendship Star block, a 6½" x 10½" dark blue-check rectangle, a dark blue-check Friendship Star block, and a 6½" dark blue square to make a pieced unit.

3. Join the 4½" x 28½" dark blue-check strip to the top of the pieced unit from step 2 to assemble the top half of Section 2.

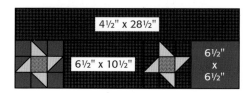

4. Join a 6½" dark blue-check square to the left edge of a dark blue Friendship Star block. Join a 4½" x 12½" dark blue rectangle to the lower edge of the pieced Friendship Star unit. Join a 10½" x 16½" speckled medium blue rectangle to the right edge of

the resulting unit to make the bottom half of Section 2.

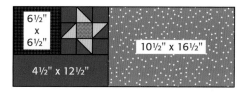

5. Join the top half of Section 2 to the bottom half.

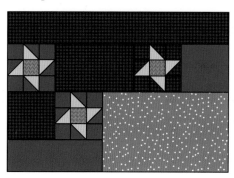

Section 2

SECTION 3

1. Follow steps 1–5 in "Making the Friendship Star Block" on page 12 to assemble 1 Friendship Star block for Section 3, substituting dark blue-check fabric for the dark blue fabric.

2. Join 2 dark blue-check 4⅞" triangles and 1 green small-check 6½" triangle to make a Flying Geese unit. Make 4 units; then join the units as shown.

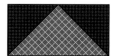

Make 4.

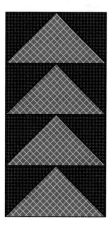

3. Join the 4½" x 8½" speckled medium blue rectangle to the top of the Flying Geese strip. Join the 4½" x 20½" speckled medium blue rectangle to the right edge of the pieced Flying Geese strip.

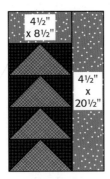

4. Join the Friendship Star block to the top of the 6½" x 14½" dark blue rectangle. Join the 16½" x 20½" dark blue rectangle to the right edge of the unit.

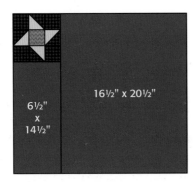

5. Join the pieced unit from step 4 to the left edge of the unit completed in step 3 to make Section 3.

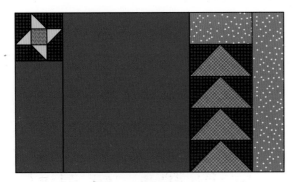

Section 3

SECTION 4

1. Join an 8½" x 13½" tan-and-green-check rectangle to each side of the 2½" x 13½" dark brown strip. Join the 11½" x 18½" tan-and-green-check rectangle to the top of this unit.

2. Join the 6½" x 24½" dark blue rectangle to the right edge of the 4½" x 24½" dark blue-check rectangle.

3. Join the tan-and-green-check unit to the right edge of the blue pieced unit to make the background for Section 4.

4. Refer to "Appliqué Instructions" on page 7 to transfer tree #1, tree #2 top and bottom, and the bear cub patterns on pages 48–53 to freezer paper and prepare the appliqué pieces. Referring to the photo on page 9 and the illustration of Section 4 below for placement, appliqué the pieces in place. Be sure that the seam allowances along the bottoms of tree #1 and tree #2 are flush with the section background, so the tree seam allowances will be concealed when the sections are joined together.

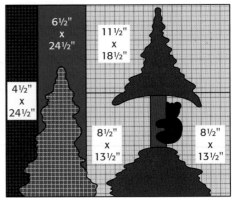

Section 4

SECTION 5

1. Transfer tree #3 on pages 52–53 to freezer paper and prepare the appliqué pieces. Referring to the photo on page 9 and the illustration below for placement, appliqué the tree to the 8½" x 14½" tan-and-green-check rectangle, aligning the lower edge of the tree appliqué with an 8½" edge on the rectangle.

2. Join a 4" x 10½" tan-and-green-check rectangle to each long edge of the 1½" x 10½" medium brown strip. Join the appliquéd tree unit to the top of this unit.

3. Join the 2½" x 24½" dark brown strip to the left edge of the tree unit.

4. Join the 10½" x 24½" salmon check rectangle to the left edge of the tree unit.

Note: Do not appliqué the moose until all the pieces of this section are sewn together.

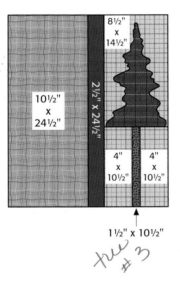

5. Working from left to right, join the following pieces together: the 4½" x 16½" medium blue-check rectangle, the 2½" x 16½" dark blue strip, the 1½" x 16½" medium brown strip, and the 1½" x 16½" dark blue strip. Join the 8½" burnt red square to the bottom of the striped unit.

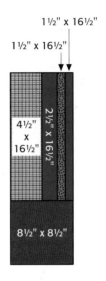

6. Join the unit from step 5 to the left edge of the tree unit from step 4 to make Section 5.

7. Transfer the large moose body, hooves, head, antlers, and eye patterns on pages 60–62 to freezer paper and prepare the appliqué pieces. Referring to the photo on page 9 and the illustration of Section 5 below for placement, appliqué the moose in place in the following order: moose body, antlers, hooves, head, and eyes. Appliqué the hooves so the bottom edges line up evenly with the bottom edge of the background unit.

Section 5

SECTION 6

Note: Do not appliqué the beaver to Section 6 until it is joined to Section 12.

MAKING THE BEAR PAW BLOCK

1. Join a black-print triangle and a burnt red 2⅞" triangle to make a half-square-triangle unit. Repeat to make 4 half-square-triangle units.

Make 4.

2. Join 2 half-square-triangle units and a 2½" burnt red square as shown.

3. Join 2 half-square-triangle units and a 4½" black-solid square as shown.

4. Join the units from steps 2 and 3 to make a Bear Paw block.

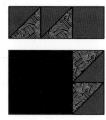

Make 1.

ASSEMBLING SECTION 6

1. Join the 2½" x 6½" rectangle from the same green as tree #3 to the left side of the Bear Paw block (toes pointing up and to the right). Join the 4½" x 8½" rectangle from the same green as tree #3 to the lower edge of the Bear Paw unit.

2. Join the 8½" x 10½" khaki green rectangle to the right edge of the Bear Paw unit.

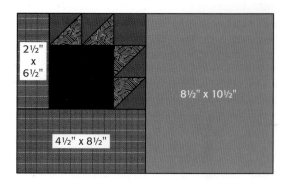

3. Join 2 green large-check 2⅜" triangles to 2 dark brown 2⅜" triangles to form a pieced square unit.

4. Join the 2½" x 3½" dark brown rectangle to the upper (brown) edge of the pieced square. Join the 2½" x 5½" dark brown rectangle to the opposite edge of the pieced square.

5. Join the 2½" x 10½" green large-check strip to the left edge of the pieced unit from step 4 and join the 8½" x 10½" green large-check rectangle to the right edge.

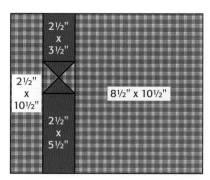

6. Join the unit from step 5 to the right edge of the Bear Paw unit from step 2 to make Section 6.

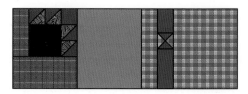

Section 6

SECTION 7

1. Make 2 Bear Paw blocks, following steps 1–4 on page 16, substituting the green large-check fabric for the burnt red.

2. Join the following pieces from left to right: the 6½" green large-check square, a Bear Paw block (toes pointing down and to the left), and the 6½" square cut from the same green as tree #4.

3. Join the 4½" x 18½" rectangle cut from the same green as tree #5 to the upper edge of the pieced unit to make the right side of Section 7.

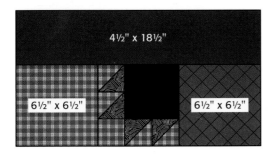

4. Join the 4½" x 6½" rectangle cut from the same fabric as tree #3 to the left edge of the remaining Bear Paw block (toes pointing up and to the left). Join the 4½" x 10½" burnt red rectangle to the lower edge of the pieced unit to make the left side of Section 7.

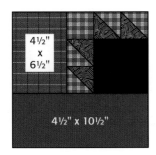

5. Join the left and right sides of the section together to complete Section 7.

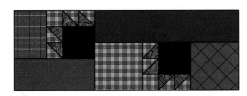

Section 7

SECTION 8

1. Tape together 6 sheets of 8½" x 11" paper horizontally, 2 down and 3 across. To make the pattern for the mountain template, draw a 15" x 30¼" rectangle on the paper; cut on the marked lines. Place the rectangle horizontally and mark a point on the right edge 1¼" from the lower right corner. Mark a point on the upper edge 13" from the upper right corner. Using the illustration on page 18 as a guide for the outline of the mountain, draw 3 to 4 mountain peaks in a continuous line. Start at the lower left corner of the rectangle, centering the largest peak at the marked point along the upper edge and ending at the marked point in the lower right corner. Using the illustration on page 23 as a guide, draw 3 snowcaps on the mountain peaks.

2. Transfer the mountain and snowcap patterns to freezer paper and prepare the appliqué pieces. Referring to the photo on page 9 and the illustration of Section 8 on page 18 for placement, appliqué the mountain to the 12½" x 30½" speckled medium blue rectangle, aligning the lower edges; appliqué the sides of the mountain only three-quarters of the way up each side. The top of the mountain and the snowcaps cannot be appliquéd into place until the mountain is attached to Section 3 in step 7 on page 22.

3. Join the 4½" x 12½" green large-check rectangle to the right edge of the mountain piece.

4. Join 2 burnt red 4⅞" triangles and a 6½" khaki green triangle to make a Flying Geese unit as in Section 3, step 2, on page 13.

5. Join the 4½" x 26½" green small-check rectangle to the left edge of the Flying Geese unit. Join the pieced unit to the lower edge of the mountain unit.

6. Join the 8½" x 16½" medium blue-check rectangle to the left edge of the mountain unit to make Section 8.

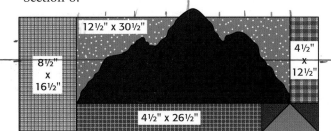
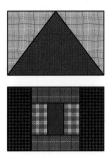

Section 8

to each side of the roof. Sew the roof unit to the lower portion of the cabin unit from step 3 to complete the Cabin block.

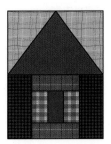

SECTION 9

MAKING THE CABIN BLOCK

1. Join a 2½" x 4½" green large-check rectangle to each side of the 2½" x 4½" rectangle cut from the same green as tree #2.

2. Join a 2½" x 6½" rectangle cut from the same green as tree #3 to the top and bottom of the pieced unit from step 1.

3. Join a 3½" x 8½" dark blue-check rectangle to each side of the pieced unit from step 2 to make the lower portion of the cabin unit.

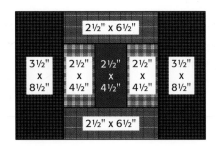

4. Cut 1 cabin roof piece from burnt red and 2 roof background pieces from salmon check, using the patterns on page 78. Join a roof background piece

ASSEMBLING SECTION 9

1. Transfer tree #4 and tree #5 on pages 54–57 to freezer paper and prepare the appliqué pieces. Referring to the photo on page 9 and to the illustration below for placement, appliqué the lower half of tree #4 to the 10½" salmon-check background square, aligning the lower edges; the top half of the tree cannot be appliquéd into place until it has been joined to Section 8 in step 3 on page 22. Appliqué tree #5 onto the 12½" x 16½" medium blue-check rectangle.

2. Join a 5" x 6½" salmon-check rectangle to each side of the 1½" x 6½" medium brown strip. Join the pieced unit to the lower edge of the tree #4 unit to complete the tree unit.

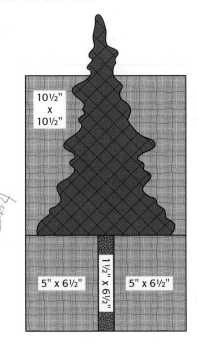

3. Join 2 burnt red 4⅞" triangles and a 6½" khaki green triangle to make a Flying Geese unit as in Section 3, step 2, on page 13. Repeat to make 2 more Flying Geese units. Join the 3 Flying Geese units together in a vertical strip; then join the 4½" x 8½" green large-check rectangle to the lower edge of the Flying Geese strip.

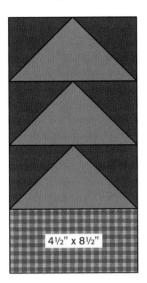

4. Working left to right, assemble Section 9 in the following order: Cabin block, tree #4, tree #5, and the Flying Geese strip from step 3.

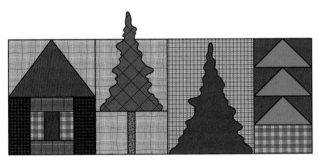

Section 9

SECTION 10

1. Join the 2½" x 8½" dark brown rectangle to the right edge of the 8½" x 27½" green small-check rectangle. Join the 8½" x 13½" green thin-stripe rectangle to the right edge of the pieced unit.

2. Tape 3 sheets of 8½" x 11" paper together vertically, 3 across. To make the pattern for the lake template, draw a 7" x 22" rectangle on the paper. Using the illustration below as a guide for the outline of the lake, draw the lake within the lines of the rectangle. Cut on the marked lines.

3. Transfer the lake pattern from step 2 and large bear pattern on page 63 to freezer paper and prepare the appliqué pieces. Referring to the photo on page 9 and the illustration below for placement, appliqué the lake to the green small-check background, and the bear to the green thin-stripe background.

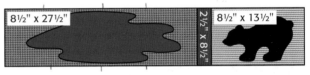

Section 10

SECTION 11

1. Join the 4½" x 13½" rectangle from the same green as tree #5 to the left edge of the 4½" green thin-stripe square.

2. Join the 4½" khaki green square to the left edge of the 4½" x 13½" rectangle from the same green as tree #1.

3. Join the lower edge of the unit from step 1 to the upper edge of the unit from step 2. Join the 8½" x 12½" medium blue-check rectangle to the right edge of the resulting unit.

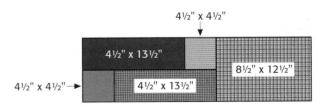

4. Working from left to right, join the following 3 pieces together: the 4½" x 12½" medium blue-check rectangle, the 4½" x 13½" khaki green rectangle, and the 4½" square from the same fabric as tree #5.

4½" x 4½"

5. Join the completed unit to the lower edge of the unit completed in step 3 to make Section 11. Refer to "Appliqué Instructions" on page 9 to transfer 3 large salmon and fins on page 58 and the large canoe pattern on page 68 to freezer paper; reverse 1 set of fins and 1 salmon. Prepare the appliqué pieces. Referring to the photo on page 9 and the illustration below for placement, appliqué the salmon to the appropriate background pieces, appliquéing the fins first, then the bodies. Appliqué the canoe to the 8½" x 12½" medium blue-check rectangle as shown.

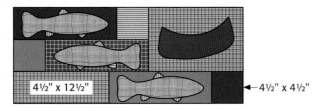

4½" x 12½"

4½" x 4½"

Section 11

SECTION 12

Note: Instructions are given for the Canadian and American flags. If you do not wish to include the Flag block, cut a 6½" x 12½" rectangle from your favorite fabric as a substitute.

CANADIAN FLAG

1. Refer to "Paper-Piecing Instructions" on pages 5–6 to construct the Leaf block. Use scraps of cream for the background and burnt red for the leaf.

2. Join the 3½" x 6½" burnt red rectangles to the right and left edges of the foundation-pieced leaf to make the Flag block.

AMERICAN FLAG

Paper-piece the flag. Use scraps of red for pieces 1, 3, and 6; scraps of white for pieces 2, 5, and 7; and a scrap of blue star print for piece 4. Join the 3½" x 6½" rectangle of your desired fabric to the right edge of the foundation-pieced flag to make the Flag block.

ASSEMBLING SECTION 12

1. Join the 2½" x 12½" green small-check strip to the lower edge of the Flag block. Join the 7½" x 8½" rectangle cut from the same green as tree #4 to the right edge of the Flag unit.

2. Join the 8½" x 14½" green thin-stripe rectangle to the right edge of the 5½" x 8½" rectangle cut from the same green as tree #3. Sew this pieced unit to the upper edge of the Flag unit.

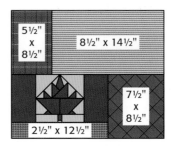

5½" x 8½"

8½" x 14½"

7½" x 8½"

2½" x 12½"

3. Join the 4½" x 6½" green thin-stripe rectangle to the 4½" x 10½" medium blue-check rectangle.

4. Join the 6½" x 16½" dark blue-check rectangle to the right edge of the pieced unit from step 3.

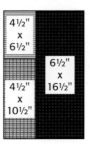

4½" x 6½"

6½" x 16½"

4½" x 10½"

5. Join the unit from step 4 to the left edge of the Flag unit completed in step 2. Transfer the small cattail flowers and leaves on page 67 and the large loon patterns on page 59 to freezer paper and prepare the appliqué pieces. Cut the cattail leaves from the same green as tree #5 and the cattail flowers from khaki green. Referring to the photo on page 9 and the illustration below for placement, appliqué the cattails to the dark blue-check background piece and the loon to the large, green, thin-stripe rectangle. With sandy green embroidery floss, embroider the stems by using a stem stitch as shown on page 8.

Section 12

SECTION 13

1. Join the 2½" x 9½" strip cut from the same green as tree #5 to the lower edge of the 9½" x 16½" burnt red rectangle. Join the 4½" x 18½" green large-check rectangle to the right edge of the unit.

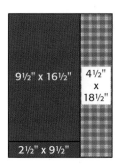

2. Join the 4½" x 13½" green small-check rectangle to the 6½" x 13½" dark blue-check rectangle. Join this pieced unit to the unit completed in step 1.

3. Transfer the large cattail flowers and leaves on pages 65–66 and 3 duckling patterns on page 57 to freezer paper, and prepare the appliqué pieces. Cut the cattail leaves from green small check, the cattail flowers from medium brown, and the ducklings from black solid. Referring to the photo on page 9 and to the illustration below, appliqué the cattail leaves and flowers to the burnt red rectangle, and the ducklings to the green small-check rectangle. With sandy green embroidery floss, embroider the stems by using a stem stitch as shown on page 8.

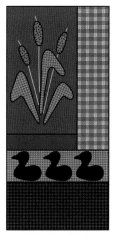

Section 13

ASSEMBLING THE SECTIONS

1. Refer to the quilt plan on page 23 and join Sections 1, 2, and 3.

2. Join Sections 4, 5, 6, and 7.

3. Join Sections 8, 9, and 10. Appliqué the top of tree #4 in Section 9 in place, with the tip extending into Section 8.

4. Join Sections 11, 12, and 13.

5. Join Section 8/9/10 to the upper edge of Section 11/12/13.

6. Join Section 4/5/6/7 to the left edge of Section 8/9/10/11/12/13. Transfer the large beaver body, paw, foot, tail, and tooth patterns on page 64 to freezer paper and prepare the appliqué pieces. Referring to the quilt plan on page 23 for placement, appliqué the beaver in place with the tail extending into Section 12.

7. Join Section 1/2/3 to the upper edge of Section 4/5/6/7/8/9/10/11/12/13. Transfer the large moon pattern on page 58 to freezer paper and prepare the appliqué piece. Referring to the quilt plan for placement, appliqué the moon over the corners where Sections 2, 4, and 8 meet. Appliqué the top of the mountain in Section 8 to the background of Section 3. Appliqué the snowcaps to the mountain peaks.

8. Sew on button eyes for the salmon, beaver, and loon.

FINISHING THE WALL HANGING

Note: Refer to "Finishing Techniques" on pages 40–45.

1. Layer the wall-hanging top with batting and backing; baste.

2. Quilt as desired.

3. Trim the batting and backing even with the top.

4. Add a hanging sleeve to the quilt, if desired.

5. Bind the edges.

"NORTH OF THE FORTY-NINE" QUEEN-SIZE QUILT

Note: You can make the wall hanging a queen-size quilt by adding two borders to the pieced top (a 3" finished inner border and a 6" finished outer border).

1. Assemble and join Sections 1–13 as indicated on pages 10–22.

2. Measure the quilt top vertically through the center. Cut two 3½"-wide inner-border strips to that measurement. Mark the centers of the border strips and the centers along the sides of the quilt top. Join the strips to the sides of the quilt top, matching centers and ends. Press seams toward the borders.

3. Measure the quilt top horizontally through the center, including the border strips just added. Cut two 3½"-wide inner-border strips to that measurement. Mark the centers of the border strips and the centers along the top and bottom edges of the quilt top. Join the strips to the top and bottom of the quilt, matching centers and ends. Press seams toward the borders.

4. Measure the quilt top vertically through the center, including the inner-border strips just added. Cut two 6½"-wide outer-border strips to that measurement. Mark the centers of the border strips and the centers along the sides of the quilt top. Join the strips to the sides of the quilt top, matching centers and ends. Press seams toward the borders.

5. Measure the quilt top horizontally through the center, including the inner-border strips just added. Cut two 6½"-wide outer-border strips to that measurement. Mark the centers of the border strips and the centers along the top and bottom edges of the quilt top. Join the strips to the top and bottom of the quilt, matching centers and ends. Press seams toward the borders.

6. Follow the finishing steps for the wall hanging.

Quilt Plan

View of the Wild by Myra Harder and Betty Klassen; Winkler, Manitoba; 28" x 36".
Bighorn sheep, found in the Canadian Rockies, inspired this quilt.

MATERIALS: 42"-WIDE FABRIC

1 fat quarter blue for sky
1 fat quarter brown for mountainside
Scraps of fabric for appliqué pieces as follows:
    3" x 5" medium brown for sheep body
    1" x 2" black for sheep hooves
    2" x 8" white for top and tip of horns
    2" x 3" light tan for sheep head
    2" x 5" white crackle for middle of horns
    2" x 3" blue for fisherman's body and arm
    2" x 2" red for fisherman's hat
    1" x 4" brown for fisherman's pole
    2" x 5" red for fisherman's canoe
    3" x 5" medium green for bush #3
    4" x 4" dark green for bush #4
    5" x 7" salmon check for salmon
    1" x 6" striped fabric for salmon fins
    4" x 8" brown for tree trunks
    14" x 8" green for 2 of tree #6
    5" x 6" green for tree #8
    6" x 7" green for tree #9
    4" x 7" green for tree #10
6" x 42" piece each of 4 light-colored fabrics for background (background A, B, C, and D)
6" x 42" piece of rust print for top and bottom borders
1 fat quarter blue for water
6" x 42" piece of dark rust for side borders
1 yd. fabric for backing
32" x 40" piece of batting
⅓ yd. fabric for binding
2 buttons, ¼" diameter, for salmon eyes
Black embroidery floss for sheep eyes

CUTTING

Note: All measurements include ¼"-wide seam allowances.

From background A, cut:
    8 squares, 4½" x 4½"

From background B, cut:
    8 squares, 4½" x 4½"

From background C, cut:
    6 squares, 4½" x 4½"
    1 rectangle, 4½" x 12½"

From background D, cut:
    8 squares, 4½" x 4½"

From the rust print, cut:
    1 rectangle, 4½" x 24½", for top border
    1 rectangle, 4½" x 8½", for bottom left border
    1 square, 4½" x 4½", for bottom right border

From the dark rust, cut:
    2 strips, 2½" x 36½", for side borders

From the blue for sky, cut:
    1 rectangle, 8½" x 12½"

From the blue for water, cut:
    1 rectangle, 8½" x 12½"

SECTION 1

1. Tape 2 sheets of 8½" x 11" paper together along an 11" edge. To make the pattern for the mountainside, draw a 7¾" x 12¼" rectangle on the paper and cut on the marked lines. Place the rectangle vertically and draw a point on the left edge ½" in from the lower left corner. Using the photo on page 24 and the illustration on page 26 as guides for the outline of the mountainside, draw a line that stairsteps from the marked point to the upper right corner of the rectangle. Cut on the marked line and discard the upper portion of the paper. The remaining paper is your mountainside pattern.

2. Refer to "Appliqué Instructions" on page 7 to transfer the following patterns on page 70 to freezer paper: sheep body and hooves; middle, top, and tip of horns; and sheep head. Also transfer the mountainside pattern from step 1 to freezer paper. Then prepare the appliqué pieces. Referring to the photo on page 24 for placement, appliqué the pieces to the 8½" x 12½" blue sky piece in the following order: mountainside; sheep body, hooves; middle, top, and tip of horns; head. Embroider the eyes of the sheep with black embroidery floss, using a satin stitch as shown on page 8 and the pattern as a guide. Stitch the line dividing the sheep legs with a running stitch.

3. Assemble the following rows from the 4½" background squares from left to right:
   Row 1: fabrics D, A, B, and D
   Row 2: fabrics C, B, C, and A
   Row 3: fabrics A, D, B, and D

4. Join Rows 1–3. Join the sheep block to the left edge of the 3-row section. Join the 4½" x 24½" top border rectangle to the upper edge of the pieced unit to make Section 1.

Section 1

SECTION 2

1. Assemble the following rows from the 4½" background squares from left to right:
   Row 1: fabrics C, A, B, C, A, and B
   Row 2: fabrics B, C, D, A, D, and C

2. Transfer the following patterns on pages 71–72 to freezer paper: fisherman's body, hat, pole, canoe, arm, bush #3, and bush #4. Prepare the apliqué pieces. Referring to the illustration of Section 2 at right for placement, appliqué the pieces in place on the 4½" x 12½" rectangle of background C.

3. Assemble Row 3 in the following order: 4½" square of background A , 4½" square of background D, appliquéd block, and 4½" square of background B.

4. Join a 4½" square of background B and a 4½" square of background A. Join the 4½" x 8½" bottom left border piece to the lower edge of the B/A unit.

5. Join the 8½" x 12½" blue water rectangle to the right edge of the pieced unit from step 4.

6. Join a 4½" square of background D and the 4½" bottom right border square. Join the pieced unit to the right edge of the water piece to complete Section 2.

7. Machine stitch the fishing line from the fishing pole to approximately the middle of the water, and curve up the end to make a hook.

8. Transfer 2 small salmon (cut 1 reversed) and fin (cut 2 sets, with 1 set reversed) patterns on page 72 to freezer paper. Prepare the appliqué pieces. Referring to the illustration below for placement, appliqué the top and lower back fins, then the salmon bodies, and finally the top front fins in place on the water background piece. Sew the two ¼"-diameter buttons into place for the fish eyes.

Section 2

9. Join Sections 1 and 2.

10. Join the 2½" x 36½" dark rust strips to the sides of the quilt top.

11. Transfer tree tops and trunk patterns for trees #8, #9, and #10 on page 76 and 2 of tree #6 on page 74 to freezer paper. Prepare the appliqué pieces. Referring to the illustration below for placement, appliqué the tree trunks and tree tops to the quilt top from right to left, in the following order: #8, #6, #10, #9, and #6. Be sure to appliqué the trunks first.

FINISHING THE WALL HANGING

Note: Refer to "Finishing Techniques" on pages 40–45.

1. Layer the wall-hanging top with batting and backing; baste.

2. Quilt as desired.

3. Trim the batting and backing even with the top.

4. Add a hanging sleeve to the quilt, if desired.

5. Bind the edges.

Evening Wilderness

Evening Wilderness by Myra Harder and Betty Klassen; Winkler, Manitoba; 40" x 20".
This hanging incorporates our favorite images from north of the forty-nine in a
different format. It's a great piece to hang over a sofa or above a mantel.

MATERIALS: 42"-WIDE FABRIC

Scraps of fabric for appliqués as follows:

- 5" x 42" tan for ground
- 3" x 5" dark tan for cliff side
- *Cabin* 3" x 4" medium red for tent front
- 4" x 4" dark red for tent side
- 7" x 8" black for bear, moose eyes and hooves, and beaver tail
- 4" x 8" brown for moose body
- 3" x 4" light brown for moose head
- 3" x 7" cream for moose antlers
- 4" x 6" brown for beaver body, paw, and foot
- 1" x 1" white for beaver tooth
- 3" x 3" yellow for moon

- 6" x 8" green for tree #6
- 5" x 7" green for tree #7
- 5" x 6" green for tree #8
- 2 different 6" x 7" greens for 2 of tree #9
- 4" x 7" green for tree #10
- 8" x 12" green for tree #11
- 5" x 10" brown for tree trunks
- ⅓ yd. fabric for background
- ½ yd. fabric for border
- ½ yd. fabric for binding and tabs (¼ yd. for each)
- ⅔ yd. fabric for backing
- 44" x 24" piece of batting
- 6 buttons, ½" diameter, for tabs

CUTTING

Note: All measurements include ¼"-wide seam allowances.

From the tan, cut:
1 strip, 2½" x 20½", for ground

From the background fabric, cut:
1 rectangle, 9½" x 36½"

From the border fabric, cut:
1 rectangle, 9½" x 40½", for top border
1 strip, 2½" x 40½", for bottom border
2 strips, 2½" x 9½", for side borders

ASSEMBLING THE WALL HANGING

1. Refer to "Appliqué Instructions" on page 7 to transfer the following patterns to freezer paper: ground, cliff side, and small bear (page 69); small beaver body, tooth, paw, foot, and tail (page 70); tent front, tent side, and small moon (page 72); small moose body, hooves, head, antlers, and eyes (page 75); trees #6 and #7 (page 74); tree #8, 2 of tree #9, and tree #10 (page 76); and tree #11 (page 77). Then prepare the appliqué pieces.

2. Join the 2½" x 20½" strip of ground to the right edge of the ground appliqué piece. Appliqué the cliff, then the ground to the 9½" x 36½" background rectangle, aligning the lower edges.

3. Sew 2½" x 9½" border strips to the left and right edges of the 9½" x 36½" background piece. Sew the 2½" x 40½" border strip to the lower edge of the background; then join the 9½" x 40½" border to the upper edge.

4. Working from right to left, stitch the remaining appliqués to the quilt top in the following order:
   Trunk and top of tree #10
   Trunk and top of tree #9
   Tent front and side
   Bear
   Trunk and top of tree #6
   Moose body, hooves, antlers, head, and eyes
   Trunk and top of tree #7
   Trunk and top of tree #8
   Trunk and top of tree #9
   Trunk and top of tree #11
   Beaver tooth, tail, body, paw, and foot
   Moon

FINISHING THE WALL HANGING

Note: Refer to "Finishing Techniques" on pages 40–45.

1. Layer the wall-hanging top with batting and backing; baste. Quilt as desired.

2. Trim the batting and backing even with the top.

3. Make and stitch 6 tabs to the upper edge. Bind the edges; then bring the tabs to the front of the wall hanging and secure in place with decorative buttons.

Black Bear Pillow

Black Bear Pillow by Betty Klassen and Meg Suderman; Winkler, Manitoba; 14" x 20".
This friendly black bear is just checking on his visitors.

MATERIALS: 42"-WIDE FABRIC

Scraps of fabric for appliqués as follows:

4" x 15" green for ground

3" x 5" light brown for cliff side

3" x 4" light red for tent front

4" x 4" dark red for tent side

6" x 8" black for bear

6" x 7" green for tree #9

5" x 7" green for tree #10

3" x 4" medium brown for tree trunks

¼ yd. or 1 fat quarter beige for background

¼ yd. or 1 fat quarter black plaid for border

½ yd. fabric for pillow backing

1 fat quarter muslin

20" x 24" piece of batting

4 buttons, 1" diameter, for pillow-back closure

CUTTING

Note: All measurements include ¼"-wide seam allowances.

From the beige, cut:

1 rectangle, 8" x 15", for background

From the black plaid, cut:

1 strip, 2½" x 8", for right border

1 rectangle, 4" x 8", for left border

1 strip, 2½" x 20½", for bottom border

1 strip, 5" x 20½", for top border

ASSEMBLING THE PILLOW

1. Refer to "Appliqué Instructions" on page 7 to transfer the following patterns to freezer paper and prepare the appliqué pieces: ground, cliff side, and small bear (page 69); tent front and side (page 72); and tree #9 and tree #10 (page 76). Referring to the photo on page 30 for placement, appliqué the cliff, then the ground to the 8" x 15" beige background rectangle, aligning the lower edges.

2. Join the 2½" x 8" border strip to the right edge of the background piece. Join the 4" x 8" border rectangle to the left edge of the background piece.

3. Join the 2½" x 20½" border strip to the lower edge of the background piece; join the 5" x 20½" border strip to the upper edge of the background piece.

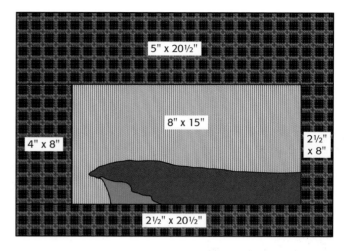

4. Working from right to left, stitch the appliqués to the pillow top in the following order: trunk of tree #10, top of tree #10, trunk of tree #9, top of tree #9, tent front, tent side, bear.

5. Using your sewing machine and dark thread, sew a line down the front of the tent to indicate a zipper line.

6. Refer to "Pillows" on pages 44–45 to complete "Black Bear Pillow."

Loon Pillow

Loon Pillow **by Cori Derksen and Betty Klassen; Winkler, Manitoba; 14" x 20".**
You may never see a loon, but you will always hear its beautiful call on quiet nights.

MATERIALS: 42"-WIDE FABRIC

⅜ yd. rust print for border and sky
⅛ yd. mottled green for water
Scraps of fabric for appliqués as follows:
  6" x 7" green for bush #1
  2" x 8" green for bush #2
  5" x 5" black solid for loon head and neck
  4" x 10" black print for loon body
  2" x 3" striped fabric for neckband
  6" x 10" green for left reed
  5" x 10" green for right reed
  7" x 11" green for middle reed
½ yd. fabric for pillow backing
½ yd. muslin
20" x 24" piece of batting
1 button, ⁵⁄₁₆" diameter, for loon eye
4 buttons, 1" diameter, for pillow-back closure

CUTTING

Note: All measurements include ¼"-wide seam allowances.

From the rust print, cut:
  1 rectangle, 2½" x 4", for right border
  1 rectangle 3½" x 4", for left border
  1 strip, 2½" x 20½", for bottom border
  1 rectangle, 9" x 20½", for sky

From the mottled green, cut:
  1 rectangle, 4" x 15½", for water

ASSEMBLING THE PILLOW

1. Join the 2½" x 4" border rectangle to the right edge of the 4" x 15½" water rectangle; join the 3½" x 4" border rectangle to the left edge of the water rectangle. Join the 9" x 20½" sky rectangle to the upper edge of the pieced unit; join the 2½" x 20½" border strip to the lower edge of the pieced unit.

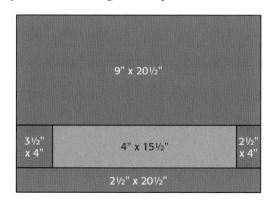

2. Refer to "Appliqué Instructions" on page 7 to transfer the following patterns to freezer paper and prepare the appliqué pieces: bush #1 (page 70); small loon head and neck, body, and neckband (page 71); left reed, right reed, and middle reed (page 73). Appliqué bush #2 approximately 2½" in from the right side, just covering the upper left edge of the water.

3. Referring to the photo on page 32 and the illustration below for placement, stitch the remaining appliqués to the pillow front in the following order: bush #1, loon head, neckband, loon body, left reed, right reed, middle reed.

4. Sew the button in place for the loon eye as indicated on the pattern.

5. Refer to "Pillows" on pages 44–45 to complete "Loon Pillow."

Moose Pillow

Moose Pillow by Cori Derksen, Betty Klassen,
and Meg Suderman; Winkler, Manitoba; 16" x 16".
When you are as big as a moose, even the trees can't hide you.

MATERIALS: 42"-WIDE FABRIC

¼ yd. blue plaid for border

⅓ yd. or 1 fat quarter navy blue print for background

Scraps of fabric for appliqués as follows:

    4" x 8" dark brown for moose body

    3" x 5" medium brown for moose head and hooves

    3" x 7" light brown for antlers

    2" x 2" black for eyes

    6" x 8" green for tree #6

    5" x 6" green for tree #7

    5" x 6" green for tree #8

    2" x 6" brown for tree trunks

    3" x 3" yellow for moon

½ yd. fabric for pillow backing

1 fat quarter muslin

20" x 20" piece of batting

5 buttons, 1" diameter, for pillow-back closure

CUTTING

Note: All measurements include ¼"-wide seam allowances.

From the blue plaid, cut:

    1 strip, 2½" x 12½", for right side border

    2 strips, 2½" x 11½", for top and bottom borders

    1 rectangle, 5½" x 16½", for left border

From the background, cut:

    1 rectangle, 9½" x 12½", for background

ASSEMBLING THE PILLOW

1. Join the 2½" x 12½" border strip to the right edge of the 9½" x 12½" background rectangle. Join the 2½" x 11½" border strips to the top and bottom edges of the pieced unit. Join the 5½" x 16½" border strip to the left edge of the pieced unit.

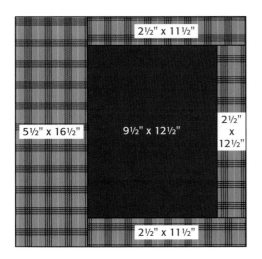

2. Refer to "Appliqué Instructions" on page 7 to transfer the following patterns to freezer paper and prepare the appliqué pieces: small moon (page 72); small moose body, hooves, head, antlers, and eyes (page 75); trees #6 and #7 (page 74), and tree #8 (page 76).

3. Referring to the photo on page 34 and the illustration below for placement, stitch the appliqués to the pillow top in the following order: moose body, hooves, antlers, head, eyes; trunk of tree #8, top of tree #8, trunk of tree #7, top of tree #7, trunk of tree #6, top of tree #6. Appliqué the moon between the background and left border 1" below the upper edge of the background piece.

4. Refer to "Pillows" on pages 44–45 to complete "Moose Pillow."

Beaver Wall Hanging

Beaver Wall Hanging by Cori Derksen and Betty Klassen; Winkler, Manitoba; 14" x 20".
This little hanging would make a great door hanger or add just
the right touch to a corner of your own cabin retreat.

MATERIALS: 42"-WIDE FABRIC

⅓ yd. brown plaid for border
⅓ yd. tan for background and tabs
Scraps of fabric for appliqués as follows:

    6 x 8" green for tree #9
    5" x 8" green for tree #10
    9" x 12" green for tree #11
    4" x 6" brown for tree trunks
    2" x 5" brown/black for beaver tail and foot
    1" x 1" cream for beaver tooth
    4" x 4" brown for beaver body and paw

1 fat quarter for backing
20" x 24" piece of batting
¼ yd. fabric for binding
Black embroidery floss
3 buttons, 1" diameter, for tabs

CUTTING

Note: All measurements include ¼"-wide seam allowances.

From the brown plaid, cut:

    1 strip, 2½" x 13", for left border
    1 strip, 3" x 11", for bottom border
    1 rectangle, 4" x 15½" for right border
    1 rectangle, 5½" x 14½", for top border

From the tan, cut:

    1 rectangle, 9" x 13", for background

ASSEMBLING THE WALL HANGING

1. Join the 2½" x 13" border strip to the left edge of the 9" x 13" background. Join the 3" x 11" border to the lower edge of the background unit. Join the 4" x 15½" border to the right edge of the background unit. Join the 5½" x 14½" border to the upper edge of the background unit.

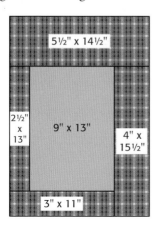

2. Refer to "Appliqué Instructions" on page 7 to transfer the following patterns to freezer paper and prepare the appliqué pieces: small beaver body, tooth, paw, foot, and tail (page 70); trees #9 and #10 (page 76); and tree #11 (page 77).

3. Referring to the photo on page 36 and the illustration below, stitch the appliqués in place in the following order: trunk of tree #10, top of tree #10, trunk of tree #9, top of tree #9, trunk of tree #11, top of tree #11; beaver tail, tooth, body, paw, and foot.

4. Embroider the beaver eye with black embroidery floss and a satin stitch, as described on page 8.

FINISHING THE WALL HANGING

Note: Refer to "Finishing Techniques" on pages 40–45.

1. Layer the wall-hanging top with batting and backing; baste.

2. Quilt as desired.

3. Trim the batting and backing even with the top.

4. Make and stitch the tabs to the upper edge of the wall hanging. Bind the edges of the wall hanging; then bring the tabs to the front of the wall hanging and secure in place with decorative buttons.

Salmon Wall Hanging

Salmon Wall Hanging **by Cori Derksen and Betty Klassen; Winkler, Manitoba; 16" x 16".**
This wall hanging was designed for Mark Harder, who is a true fisherman at heart.

MATERIALS: 42"-WIDE FABRIC

⅓ yd. blue-and-green plaid for border
⅓ yd. blue for water and tabs
Scraps of fabric for appliqués as follows:
    2" x 2" yellow for fisherman's hat
    2" x 3" blue for fisherman's body and arm
    1" x 4" brown for fisherman's pole
    2" x 5" red for fisherman's canoe
    6" x 7" salmon check for salmon bodies
    2" x 6" striped fabric for fins
    3" x 5" green for bush #3
    4" x 4" green for bush #4
1 fat quarter muslin for backing
20" x 20" piece of batting
¼ yd. fabric for binding
2 buttons, ⅜" diameter, for fish eyes
3 buttons, 1" diameter, for tabs

CUTTING

Note: All measurements include ¼"-wide seam allowances.

From the blue-and-green plaid, cut:
    1 rectangle, 3" x 8", for right border
    1 rectangle, 3½" x 8", for left border
    1 strip, 2½" x 16½", for bottom border
    1 rectangle, 7" x 16½", for top border

From the blue, cut:
    1 rectangle, 8" x 11", for water

ASSEMBLING THE WALL HANGING

1. Join the 3" x 8" border rectangle to the right edge of the 8" x 11" water rectangle. Join the 3½" x 8" border rectangle to the left edge of the pieced unit. Join the 2½" x 16½" border strip to the lower edge of the pieced unit.

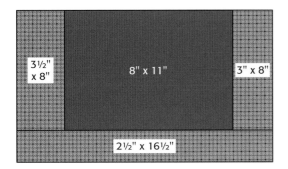

2. Refer to "Appliqué Instructions" on page 7 to transfer the following patterns on page 72 to freezer paper and prepare the appliqué pieces: fisherman's hat, body, arm, pole, canoe, 2 small salmon (cut 1 reversed), fins (cut 2 sets, with 1 set reversed). Then transfer and prepare bush #3 and bush #4 on page 71.

3. Appliqué bush #4 to the 7" x 16½" top border rectangle, 2¼" in from the right edge, aligning the lower edges. Appliqué bush #3 to the top border 1¾" in from the left edge, aligning the lower edges.

4. Pin the canoe and fisherman appliqués evenly between the 2 bushes, aligning the canoe with the lower edge of the border piece. Stitch the appliqués in place in the following order: fisherman's body, hat, pole, arm, and canoe.

5. Join the appliquéd top border piece to the upper edge of the pieced unit from step 1.

6. Using a sewing machine and light thread, sew a line down from the top of the fishing pole to just past halfway down the water rectangle; curve up the end to make a hook.

7. Pin the 2 salmon and their fins into place. Appliqué the top and lower back fins, then the salmon bodies, and finally the lower front fins.

8. Sew the 2 buttons to the salmon for eyes.

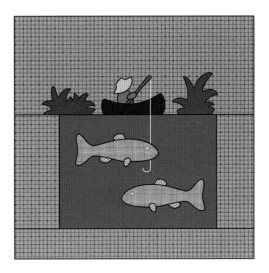

FINISHING THE WALL HANGING

Note: Refer to "Finishing Techniques" below.

1. Layer the wall-hanging top with batting and backing; baste.

2. Quilt as desired.

3. Trim the batting and backing even with the top.

4. Make and stitch the tabs to the upper edge of the wall hanging.

5. Bind the edges.

6. Bring the tabs to the front of the wall hanging and secure in place with decorative buttons.

Finishing Techniques

ASSEMBLING THE LAYERS

Once the project top is finished, you will need to layer it with the batting and backing before you quilt it unless you are making a pillow and prefer not to quilt it (see "Pillows"on pages 44–45). To assemble the layers, follow these steps:

1. Mark the quilt top with the desired quilting design.

2. The project instructions in this book specify to cut the batting 4" larger than the pieced top. This allows 2" extra on each side for the take-up that occurs during quilting. Cut the backing fabric to the same size as the batting, piecing as necessary.

3. Place the backing, right side down, on a flat surface. Using masking tape, secure it in several places along the edges. Make sure the backing is smooth and taut. Position the batting over the backing and smooth it into place. Center the pieced top, right side up, over the batting and backing.

4. Working from the center out, baste the layers together with thread or safety pins.

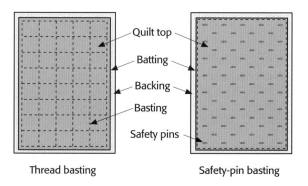

Thread basting   Safety-pin basting

QUILTING

These wilderness projects lend themselves very nicely to many quilting techniques and patterns. Although we love finishing a project with hand quilting, you can add quilting stitches either by hand or machine. The big open areas of "North of the Forty-Nine" are the perfect places for creative quilting. The sky areas in the designs also provide an opportunity for interesting quilting designs. We used freehand swirls to create movement in "Black Bear Pillow" on page 30. For water, we often quilt wavy lines for interest. The animals, trees, and other objects are simply outline quilted.

Let fabrics such as plaids work for you. By following the lines of the fabric, you can make interesting patterns without using quilting templates.

ADDING A HANGING SLEEVE OR TABS

At this point, if you've made a wall hanging, you'll want some way to hang it. We've found that a hanging sleeve added to the back of the quilt, or tabs stitched to the top of the quilt, will work well for the projects in this book. Each individual project will specify the method used for the project shown, but feel free to modify the hanging method to your own liking.

Hanging Sleeve

We like to add a hanging sleeve to the back of our projects before we bind the quilt. It saves on hand stitching and results in a neater-looking finish, even if it is on the back.

1. Cut a strip of fabric that is 6" wide and has a length that is 1" less than the width of the finished project.

2. Press up each end of the strip ¼", press up ¼" again, and stitch in place.

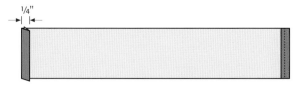

3. Fold the strip in half lengthwise, wrong sides together. Baste the raw edges together to form a tube.

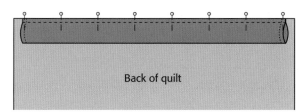

4. Center the raw edge of the strip along the top edge of the quilt back. Pin the sleeve in place.

Back of quilt

5. Bind the quilt as instructed in "Binding" on pages 42–44, securing the sleeve in the seam.

6. After the binding is folded to the back and hand stitched in place, slipstitch the bottom of the sleeve to the quilt backing. Be careful not to stitch through to the front of the quilt.

Tabs

If you have a decorative or unique rod that complements the project, tabs are an ideal way to let it shine through.

1. Using the pattern on page 42, refer to the project instructions for the required number of tabs.

2. Place 2 tabs right sides together. Stitch down one long edge, across the point, and up the remaining long edge. Leave the straight end open. Trim across the points and corners. Turn the tab to the right side; press. Repeat for each additional tab.

3. Evenly space the tabs across the wall hanging back, aligning the tab raw ends with the wall-hanging raw edge. Leave an equal amount of distance from each end. Pin or baste the tabs in place.

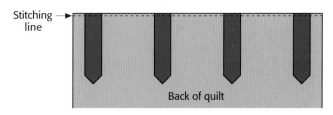

Stitching line

Back of quilt

4. Bind the wall hanging as instructed in "Binding" on pags 42–44, securing the tabs in the seam.

5. Fold each tab to the wall-hanging front, creating a loop wide enough for the rod to fit through. Secure the tabs in place by sewing a decorative button to the tab point through all of the layers.

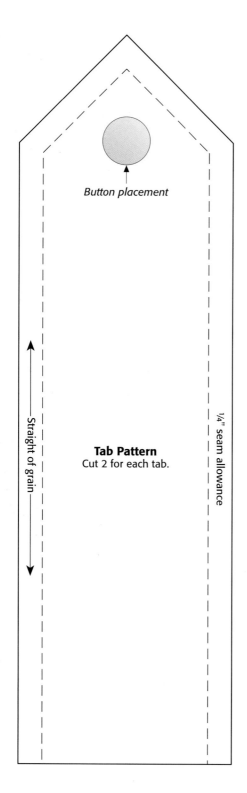

Button placement

Straight of grain

¼" seam allowance

Tab Pattern
Cut 2 for each tab.

BINDING

Binding is the most common way to finish the edges of quilts. The binding we are accustomed to using is often referred to as double binding because it is folded in half before it is stitched onto the edges. It is an easy binding for finishing your project.

1. Cut 2"-wide strips the width of your fabric. You will need enough strips to go around the perimeter of the quilt, plus 10" for the seams and the corners in a mitered fold.

2. To stitch the strips together so they are long enough to go around the project, place 2 strips right sides together so they are perpendicular to each other as shown. Draw a diagonal line on the top strip that extends from the point where the upper edges meet to the opposite point where the lower edges meet. Stitch along this line.

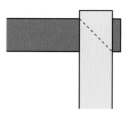

3. Trim the seam allowances to ¼". Press the seam allowances open. Add the remaining strips in the same manner.

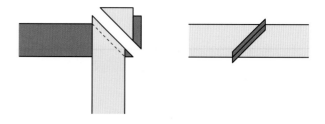

4. When all of the strips have been added, cut one end at a 45° angle. This will be the beginning of the strip. Press the binding in half lengthwise, wrong sides together, aligning the raw edges.

5. Beginning with the angled end, place the binding strip along one edge of the right side of the quilt top, aligning the raw edges. Do not start near a corner. Leaving the first 8" of the binding unstitched, stitch the binding to the quilt. Use a ¼" seam allowance. Stop stitching ¼" from the corner. Backstitch and remove the quilt from the machine.

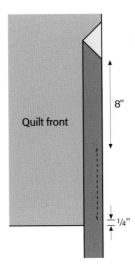

6. Turn the project so you are ready to sew the next side. Fold the binding up so it creates a 45° angle fold.

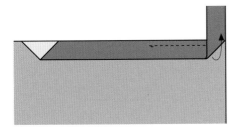

7. Place your finger on the fold to keep it in place; then fold the binding back down so the new fold is even with the top edge of the quilt and the raw edges of the binding are aligned with the side of the quilt. Beginning at the folded edge, stitch the binding to the quilt, stopping ¼" from the next corner. Repeat the folding and stitching process for each corner.

8. When you are 8" to 12" away from your starting point, stop stitching and remove the quilt from the machine. Cut the end of the binding strip so it overlaps the beginning of the binding strip by at least 5". Pin the ends together 3½" from the starting point. Clip the binding raw edges at the pin, being careful not to cut past the seam allowance or into the quilt layers. Open up the binding and match the ends as shown. Stitch the ends together on the diagonal.

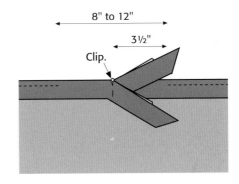

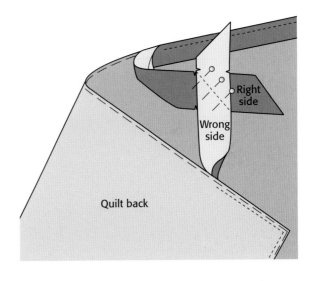

9. Refold the binding and check to make sure it fits the quilt. Trim the binding ends to ¼" from the stitching. Finish stitching the binding to the edge of the quilt.

10. Fold the binding over the raw edges to the back of the project. Slipstitch the binding to the backing along the fold, mitering the corners.

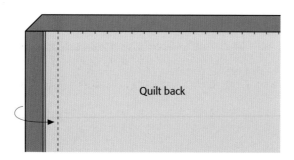

Quilt back

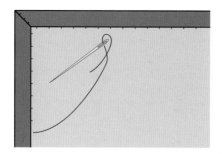

PILLOWS

Choosing to quilt your pillow top is a personal choice. Each of the pillow projects in this book lists the amount of batting and muslin required if you choose to quilt the project top. For a quilted top, follow the instructions for "Assembling Layers" and "Quilting" on pages 40–41; then complete as indicated below. If you like the unquilted look, simply disregard the requirements for the batting and muslin backing and finish as below.

FINISHING AS A SQUARE PILLOW

1. For the pillow back, cut one 3½" x 16½" rectangle and one 16½" x 16½" square.

2. Press under ¼" on a 16½" edge of the backing square. Then press under 1" on the same edge. Stitch close to the first pressed edge. Make 5 evenly spaced 1"-long buttonholes parallel to the hemmed edge.

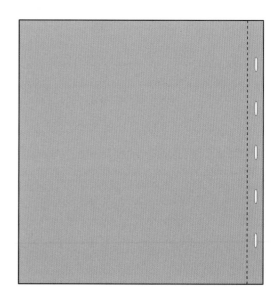

3. Press under ½" on one long edge of the 3½" x 16½" backing rectangle. Then press under ½" on the same edge. Stitch close to the first pressed edge. Position the buttons on the hemmed edge to correspond to the buttonholes on the large pillow-back piece. Stitch the buttons in place.

4. Button the pillow-back pieces together. Pin the pillow front and back wrong sides together. Stitch ¼" from the outer edges.

5. Unbutton the pillow back, turn right side out, and insert the pillow form. Button the back.

FINISHING AS A RECTANGULAR PILLOW

1. For the pillow back, cut one 3½" x 14½" rectangle and one 14½" x 20½" rectangle.

2. Press under ¼" on the 14½" edge of the large pillow-back piece. Then press under 1" on the same edge. Stitch close to the first pressed edge. Make 4 evenly spaced buttonholes, 1" in length, parallel to the hemmed edge.

3. Press under ½" on the long edge of the 3½" x 14½" backing rectangle. Then press under ½" again. Stitch close to the first pressed edge. Position the buttons on the hemmed edge to correspond to the buttonholes on the large pillow-back piece. Stitch the buttons in place.

4. Button the pillow-back pieces together. Pin the pillow front and back wrong sides together. Stitch ¼" from the outer edges.

5. Unbutton the pillow back, turn right side out, and insert the pillow form. Button the back.

SIGNING YOUR QUILT

Your quilt is not finished unless it is signed. You may think this is unnecessary and a time-consuming step, but you will thank yourself for it later. As hard as we try, we often forget when we completed a project. So find yourself a permanent marking pen and make sure you put the following information onto a label:

Made by:
Address:
Date started:
Date completed:
Any special occasion or reason for making the quilt: It will not take long before you will appreciate taking the time to include this information on your finished project.

my pillow =
unfinished 18¼ x 24

so need 1- 3½ x 18¼
+ 1 - 18¼ x 24

Patterns

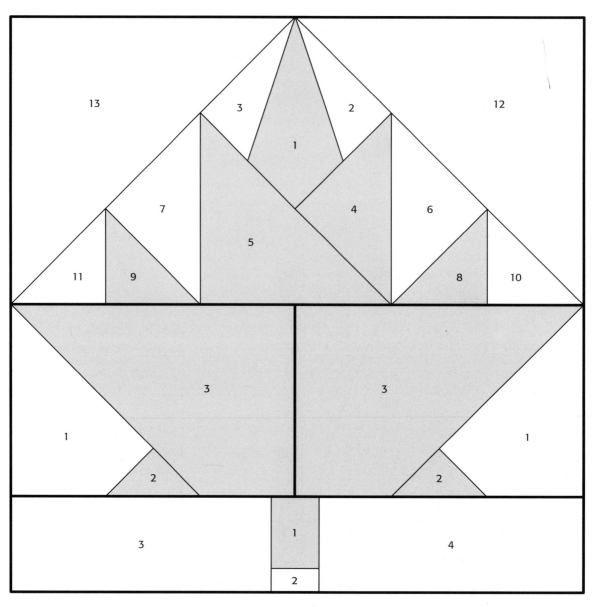

Canadian Flag

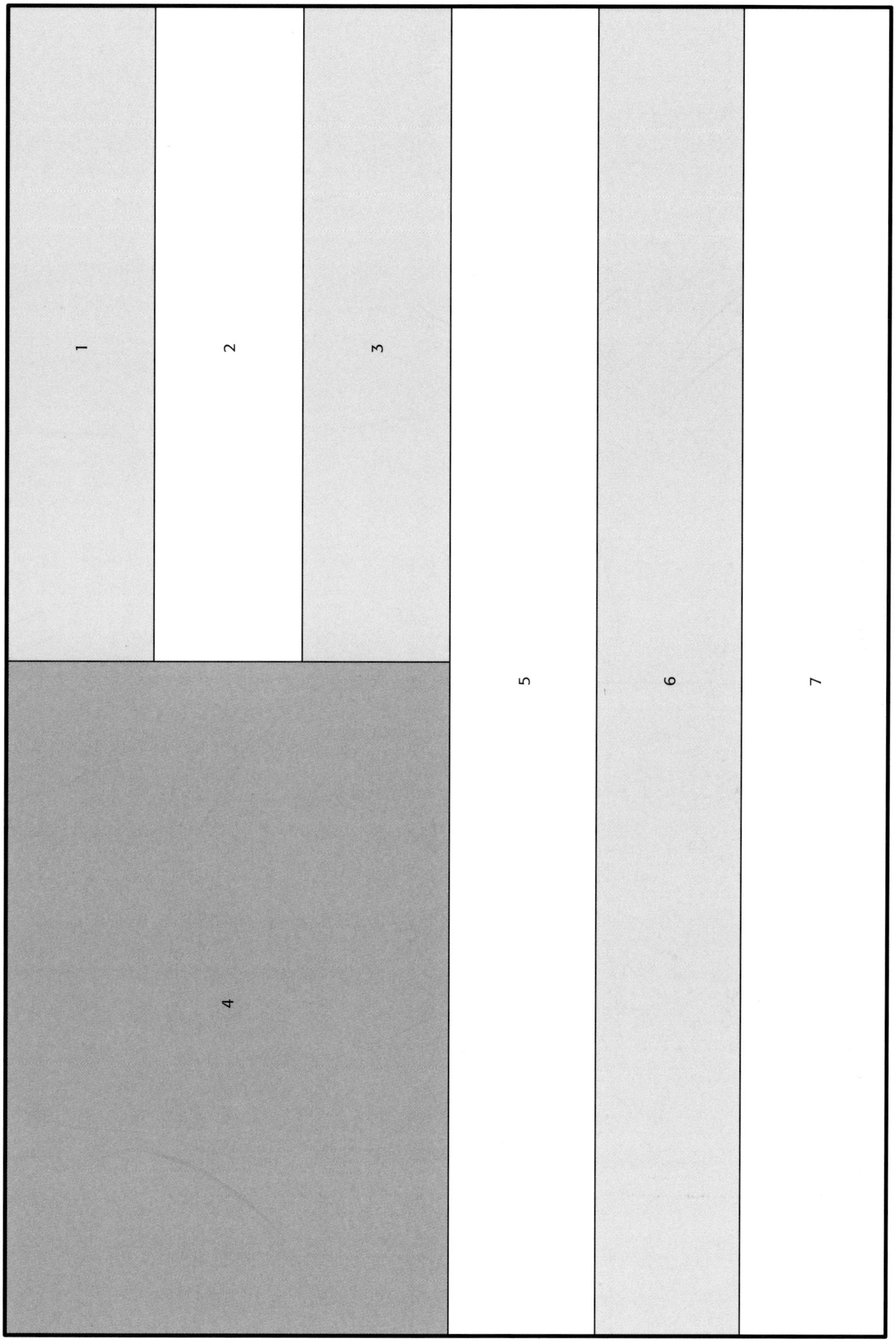

1

2

3

4

5

6

7

American Flag

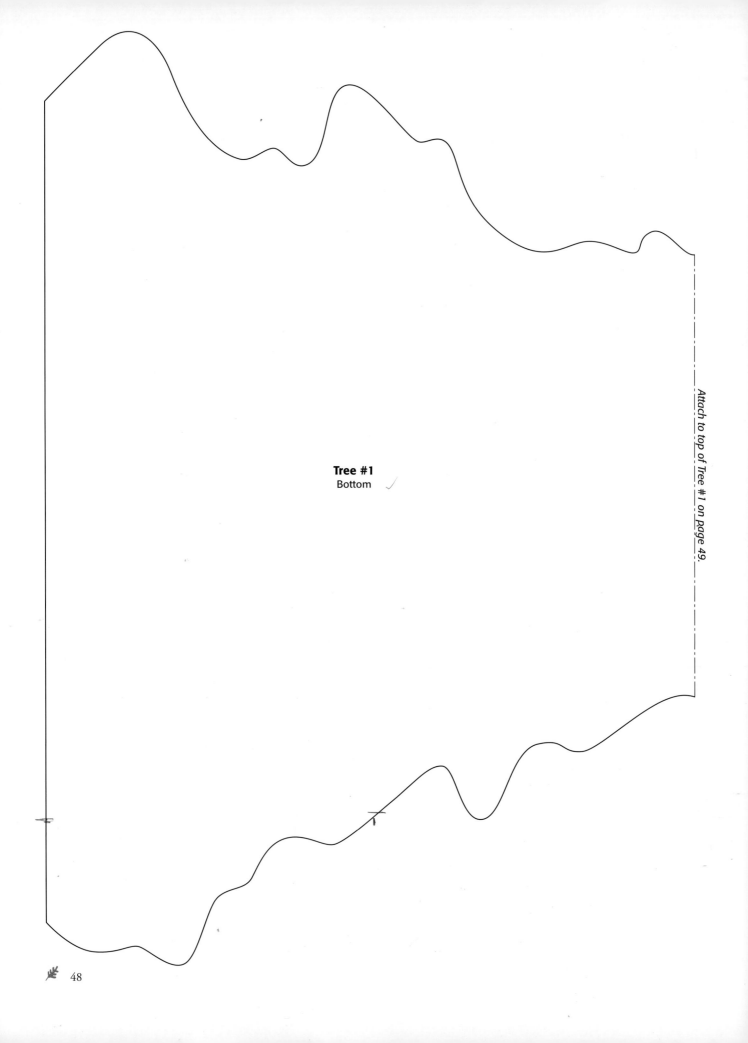

Tree #1
Bottom

Attach to top of Tree #1 on page 49.

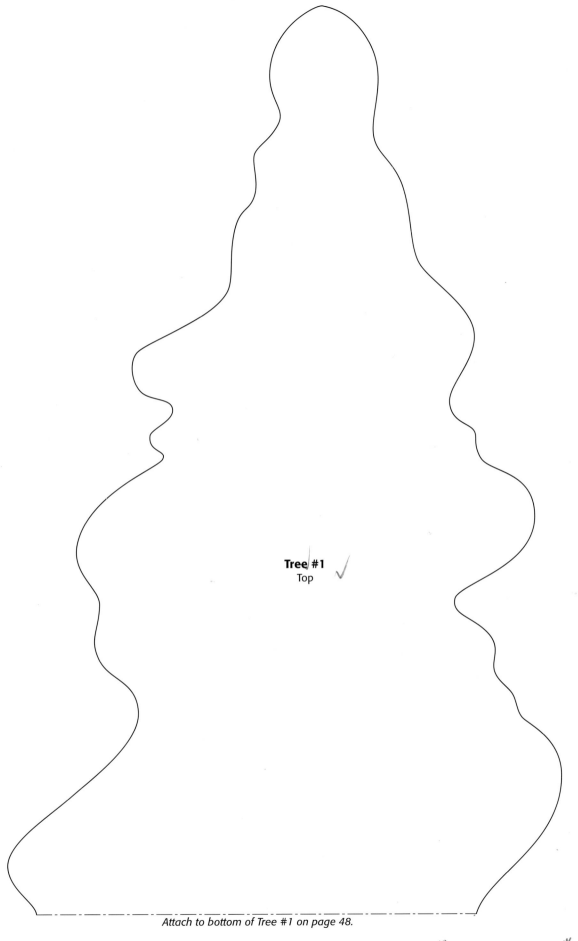

Tree #1
Top

Attach to bottom of Tree #1 on page 48.

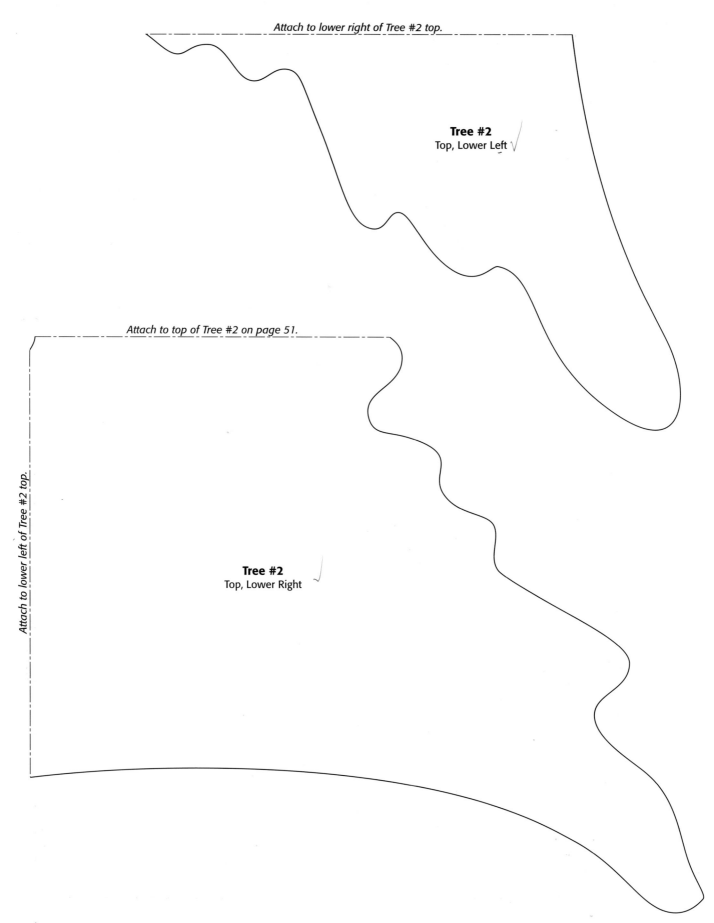

Attach to lower right of Tree #2 top.

Tree #2
Top, Lower Left

Attach to top of Tree #2 on page 51.

Attach to lower left of Tree #2 top.

Tree #2
Top, Lower Right

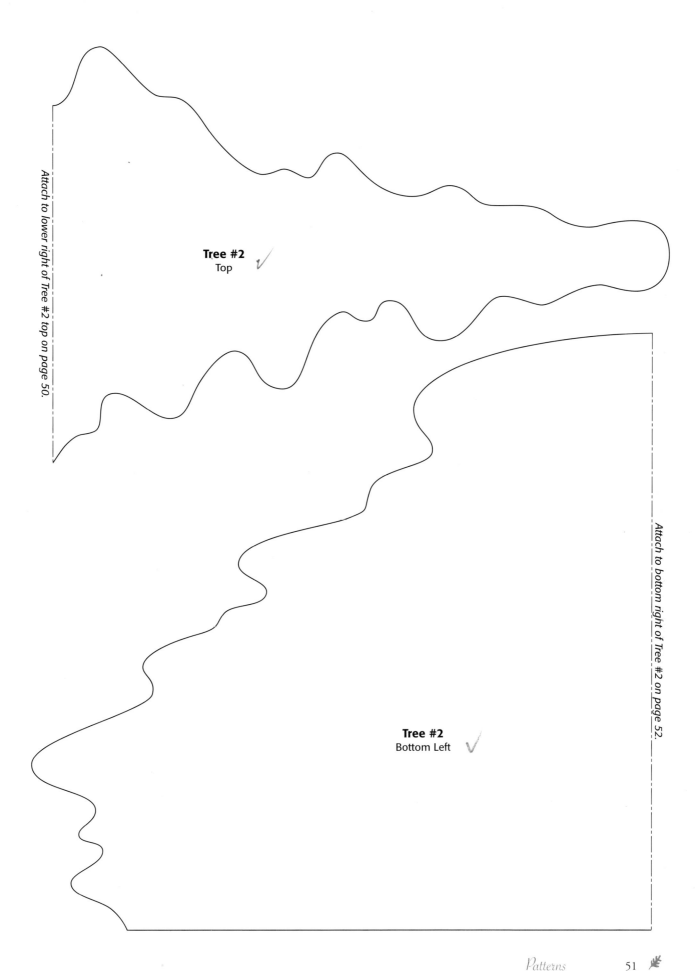

Attach to lower right of Tree #2 top on page 50.

Tree #2
Top

Tree #2
Bottom Left

Attach to bottom right of Tree #2 on page 52.

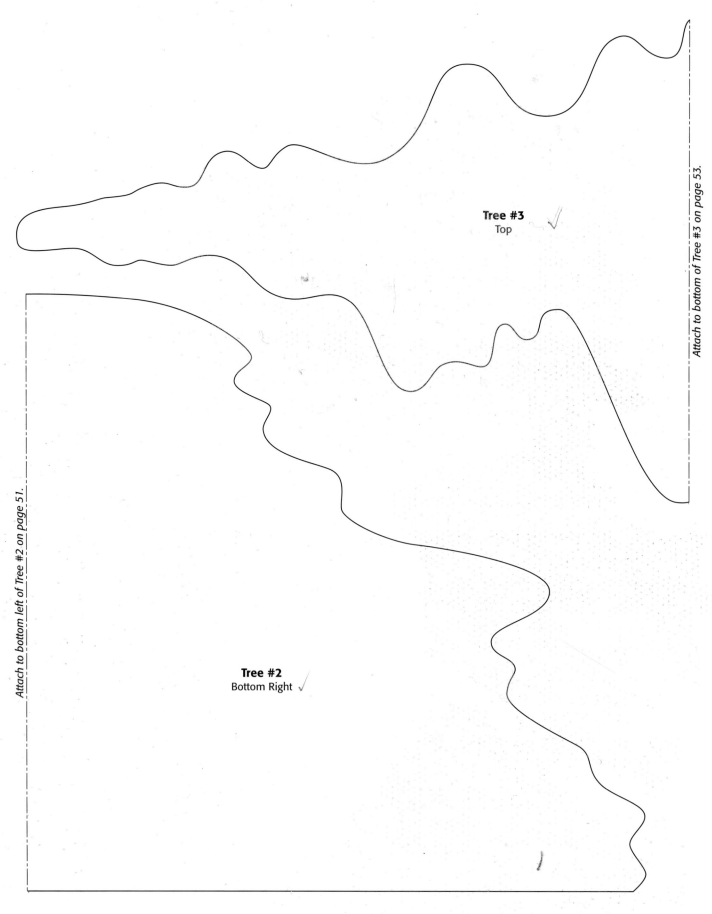

Tree #3
Top

Attach to bottom of Tree #3 on page 53.

Attach to bottom left of Tree #2 on page 51.

Tree #2
Bottom Right

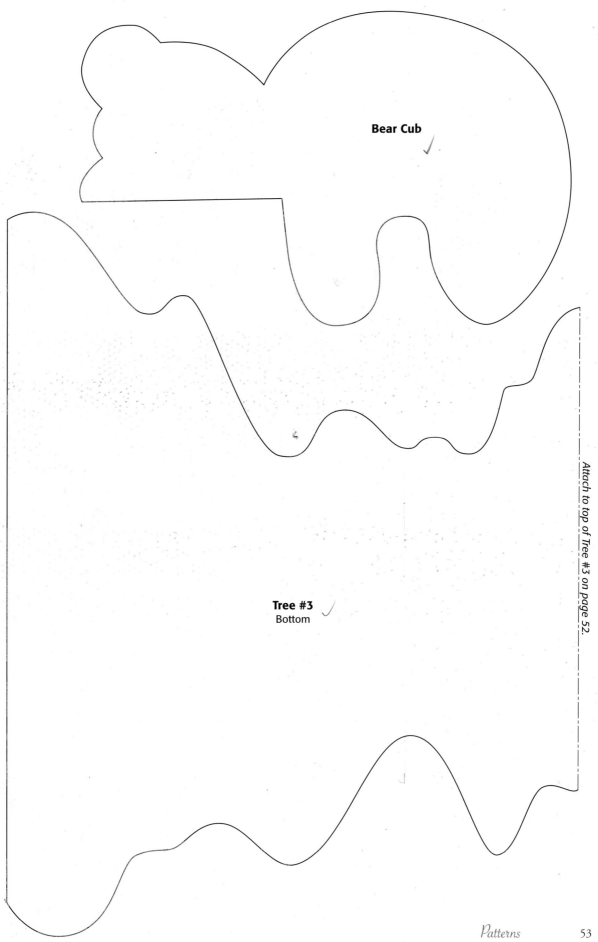

Bear Cub

Tree #3
Bottom

Attach to top of Tree #3 on page 52.

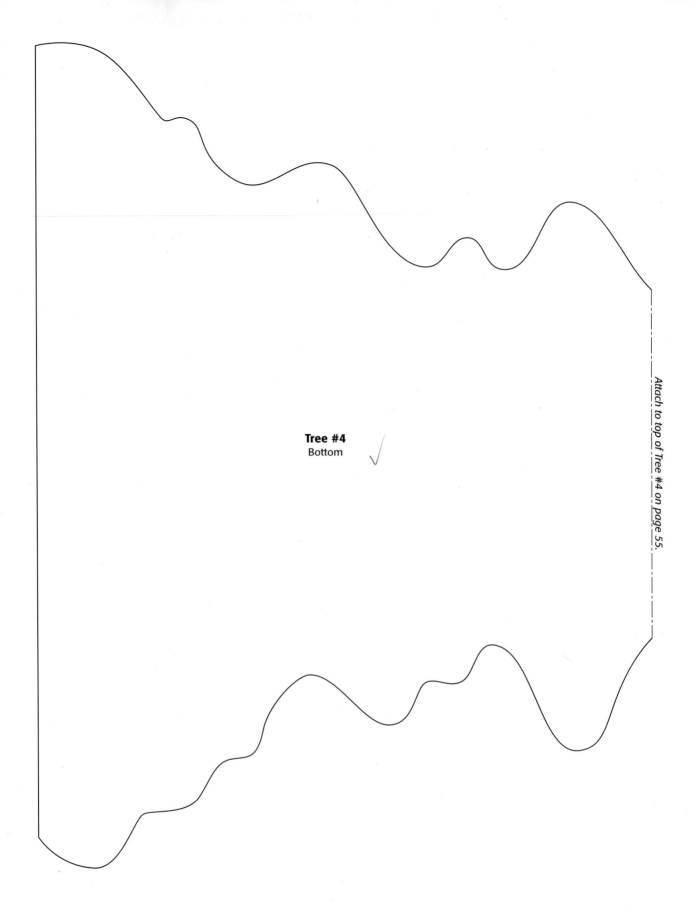

Tree #4
Bottom

Attach to top of Tree #4 on page 55.

Patterns

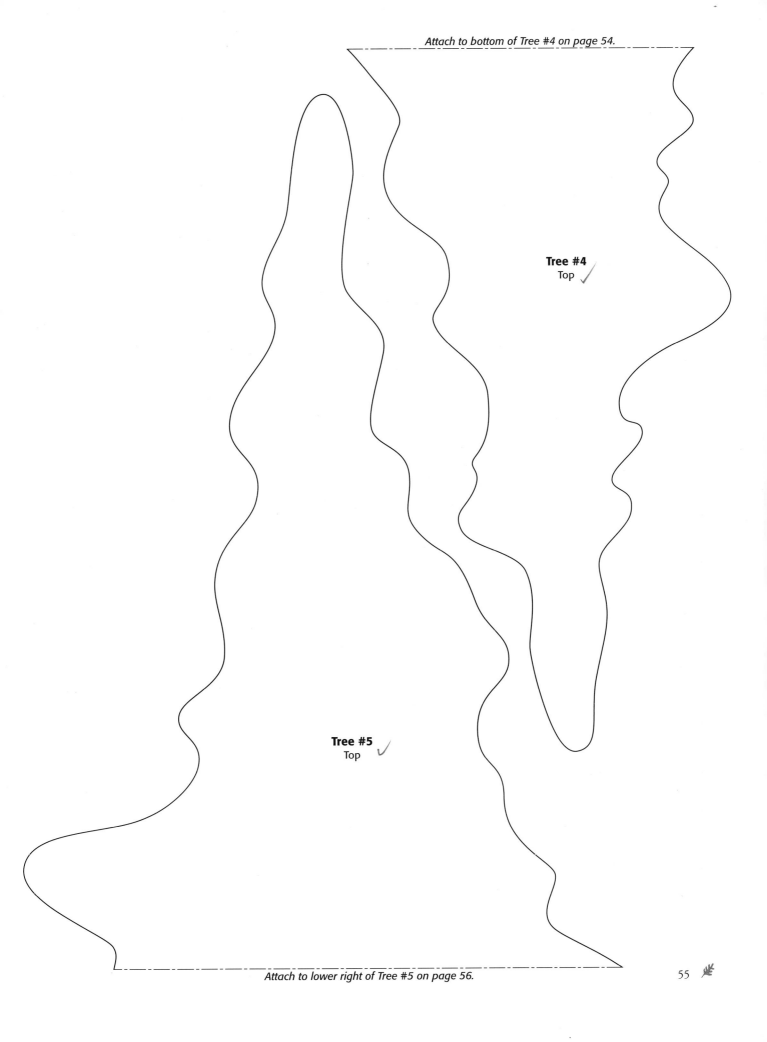

Attach to bottom of Tree #4 on page 54.

Tree #4
Top

Tree #5
Top

Attach to lower right of Tree #5 on page 56.

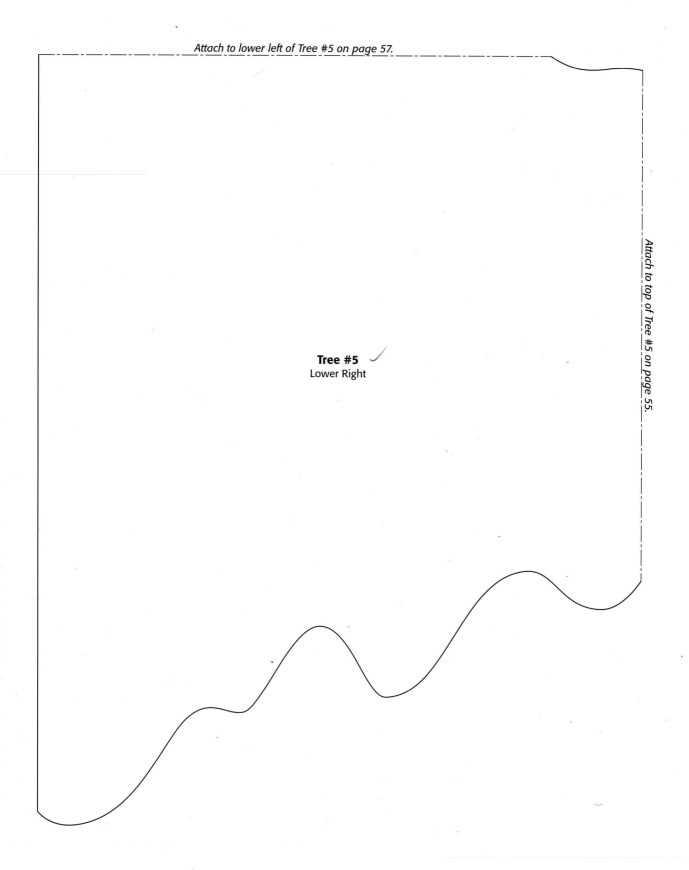

Attach to lower left of Tree #5 on page 57.

Attach to top of Tree #5 on page 55.

Tree #5
Lower Right

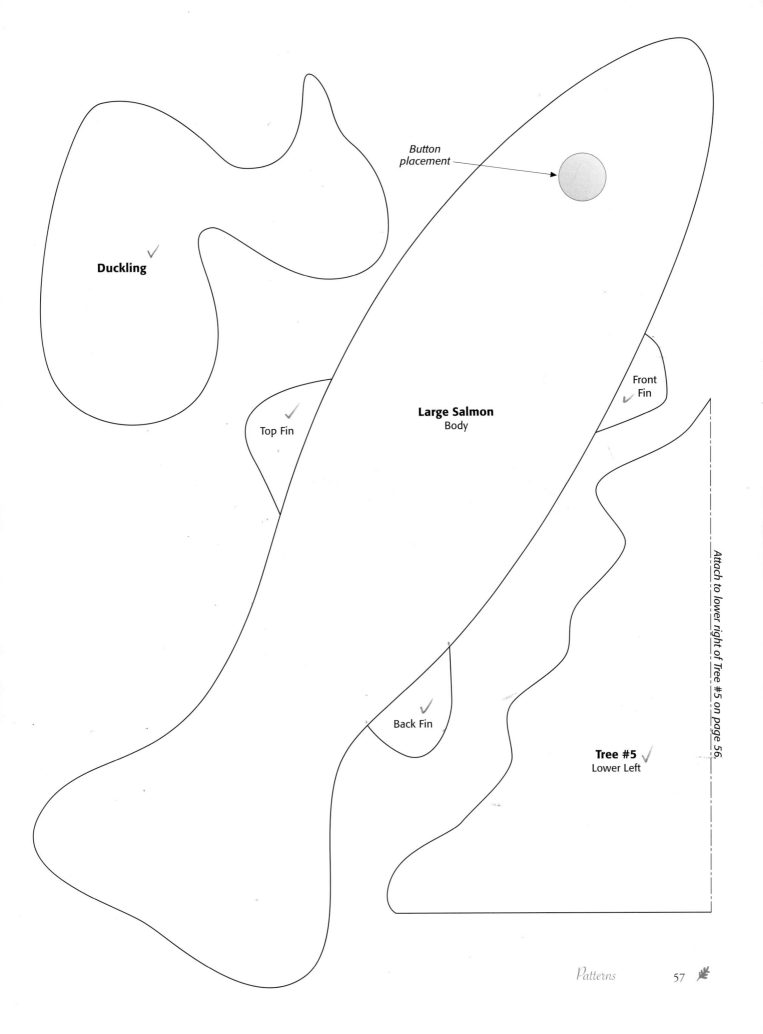

Duckling ✓

Button placement

Large Salmon
Body

Top Fin ✓

Front Fin ✓

Back Fin ✓

Tree #5 ✓
Lower Left

Attach to lower right of Tree #5 on page 56.

Large Moon

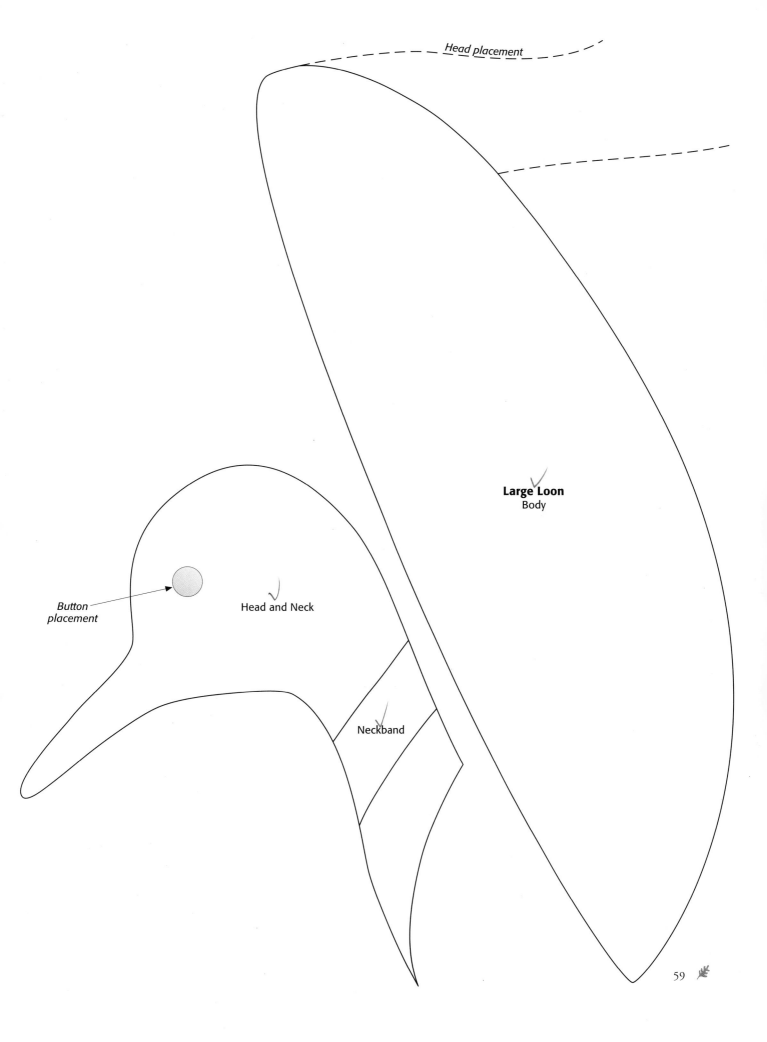

Head placement

Large Loon
Body

Button placement

Head and Neck

Neckband

Large Moose
Body Top

*Attach to Large Moose
body bottom on page 61.*

*Attach to Large Moose
body top on page 60.*

Large Moose
Body Bottom

Hoof

Hoof

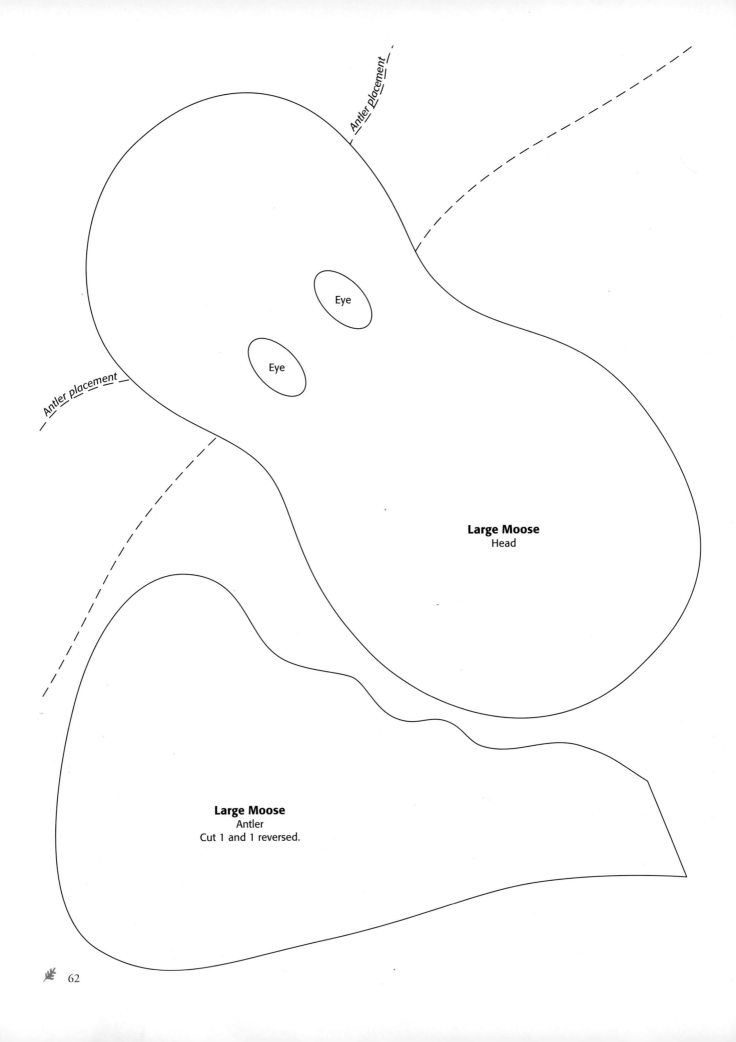

Antler placement

Antler placement

Eye

Eye

Large Moose
Head

Large Moose
Antler
Cut 1 and 1 reversed.

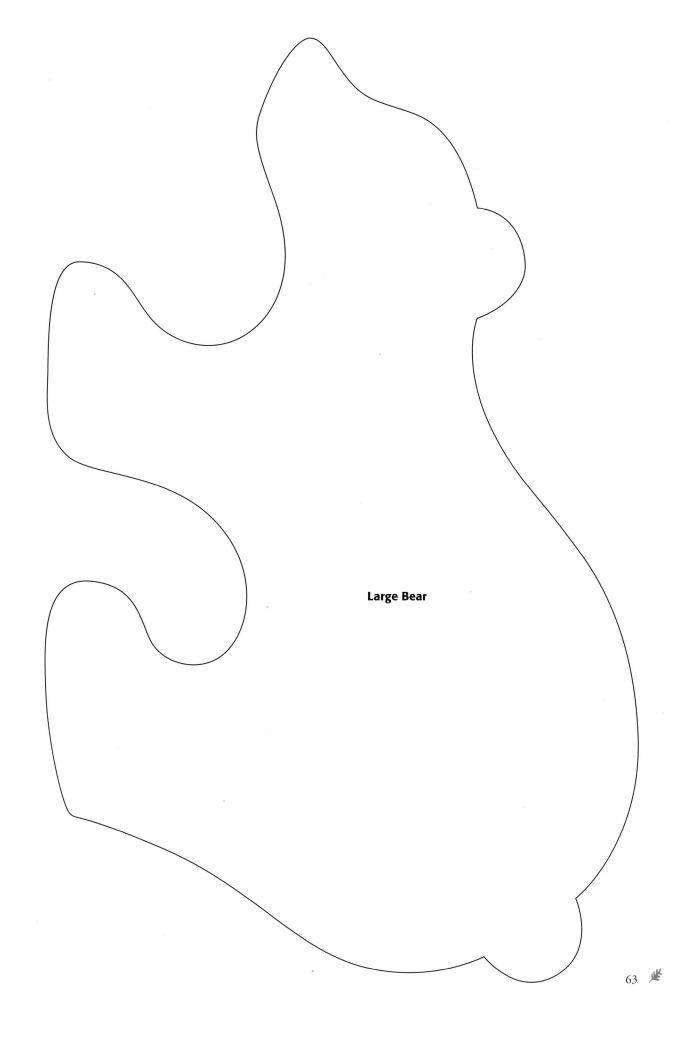

Large Bear

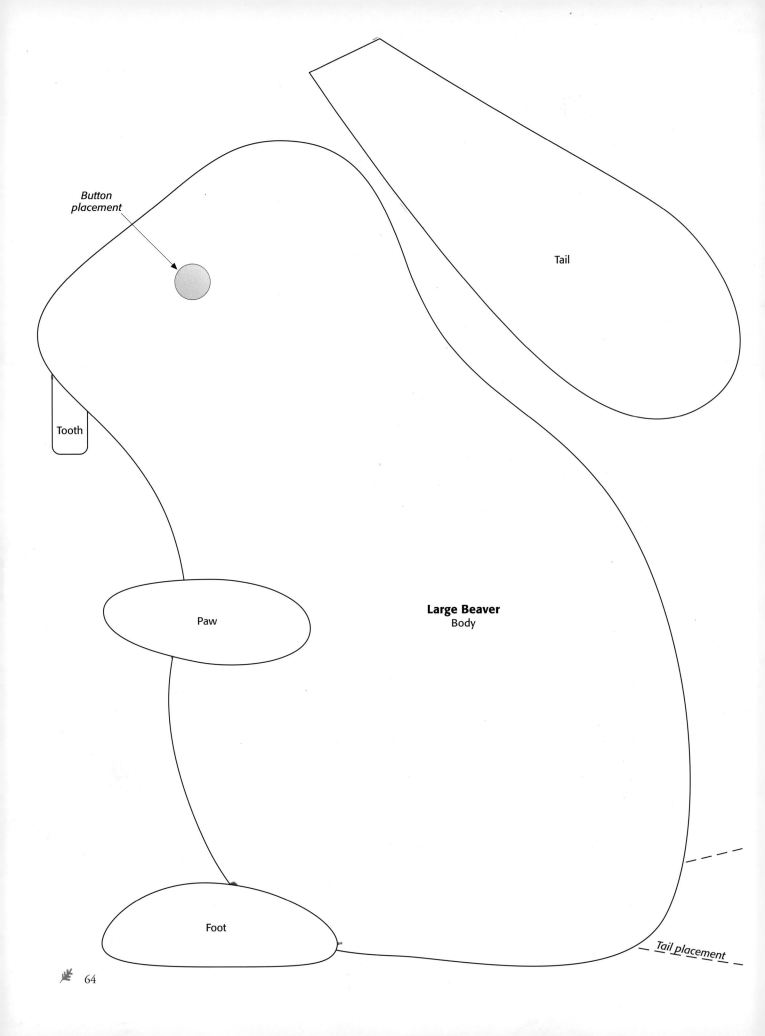

Button
placement

Tail

Tooth

Paw

Large Beaver
Body

Foot

Tail placement

64

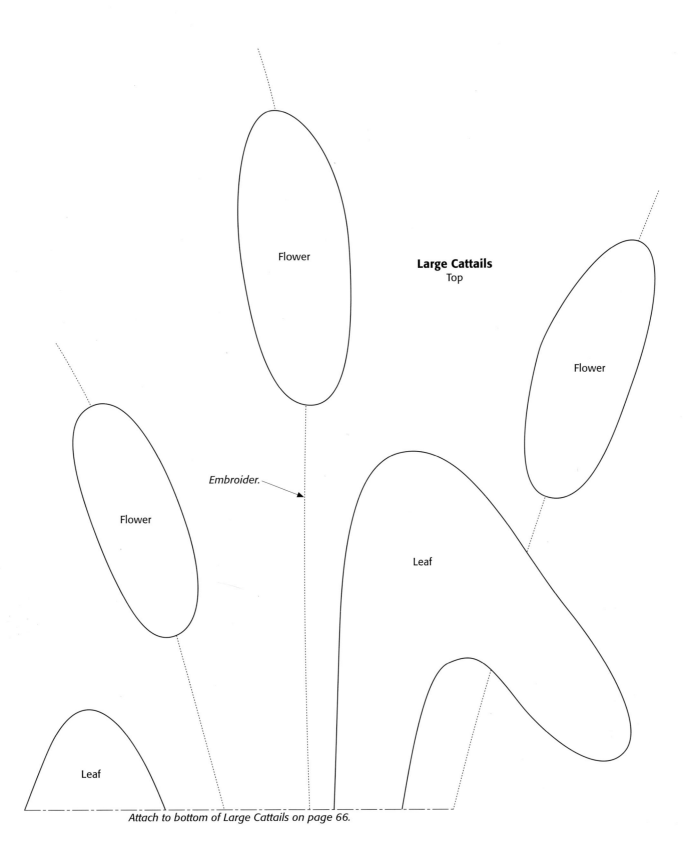

Flower

Large Cattails
Top

Flower

Flower

Embroider.

Leaf

Leaf

Attach to bottom of Large Cattails on page 66.

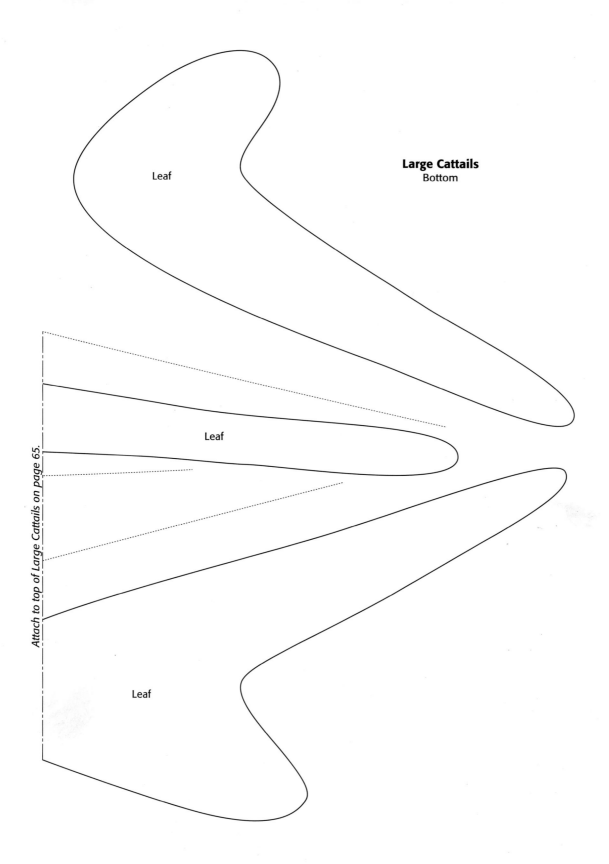

Leaf

Large Cattails
Bottom

Leaf

Attach to top of Large Cattails on page 65.

Leaf

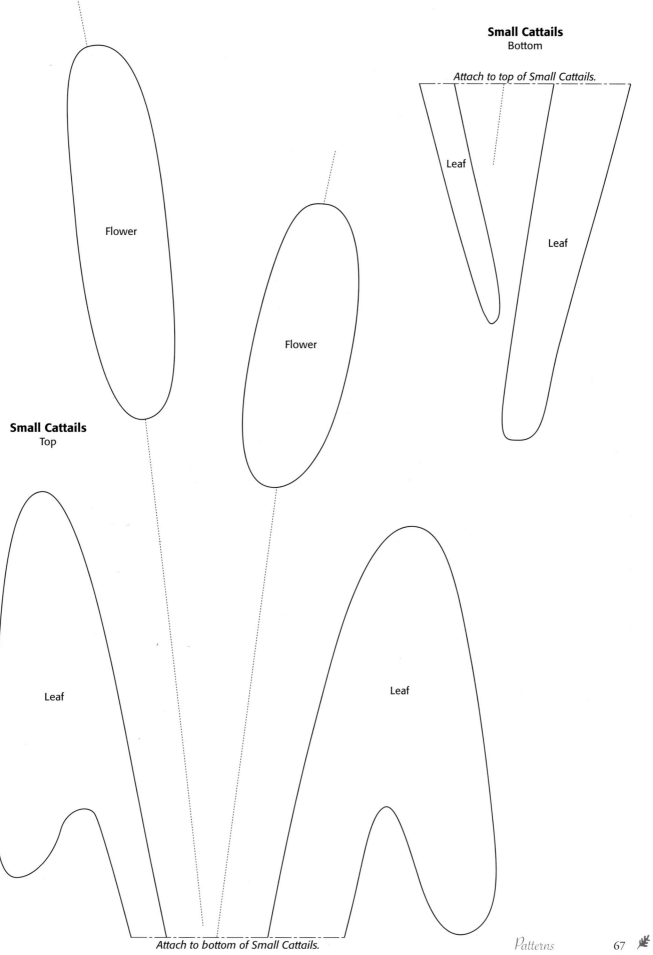

Small Cattails
Bottom

Attach to top of Small Cattails.

Leaf

Leaf

Flower

Flower

Small Cattails
Top

Leaf

Leaf

Attach to bottom of Small Cattails.

Patterns   67

Large Canoe

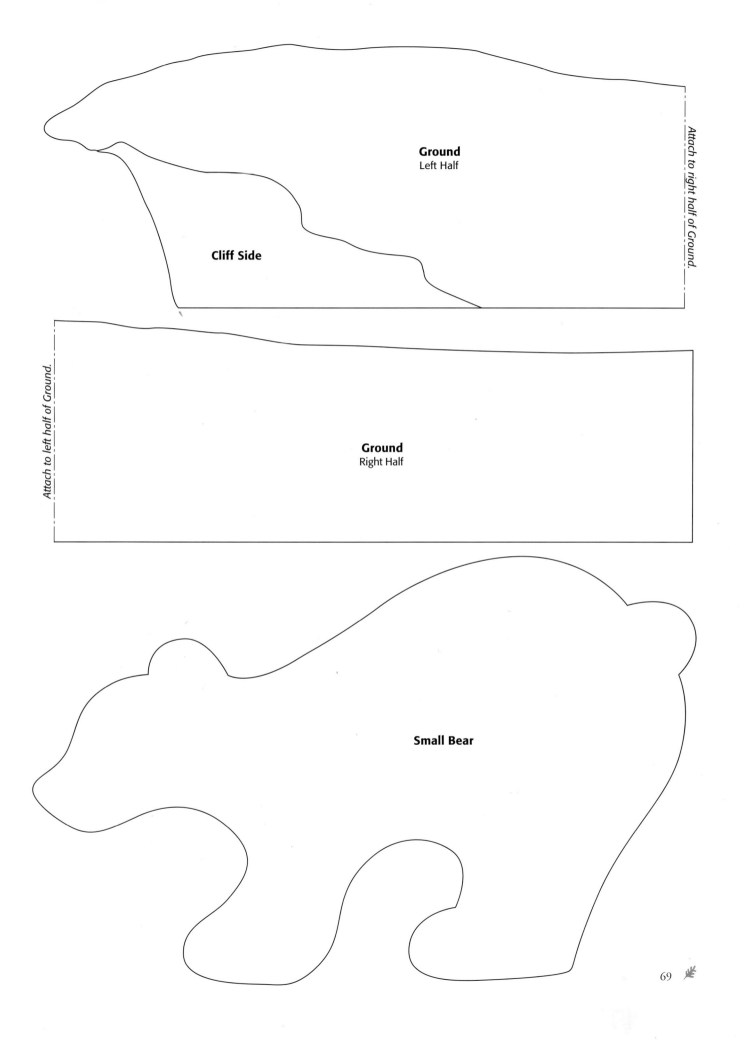

Ground
Left Half

Cliff Side

Attach to right half of Ground.

Attach to left half of Ground.

Ground
Right Half

Small Bear

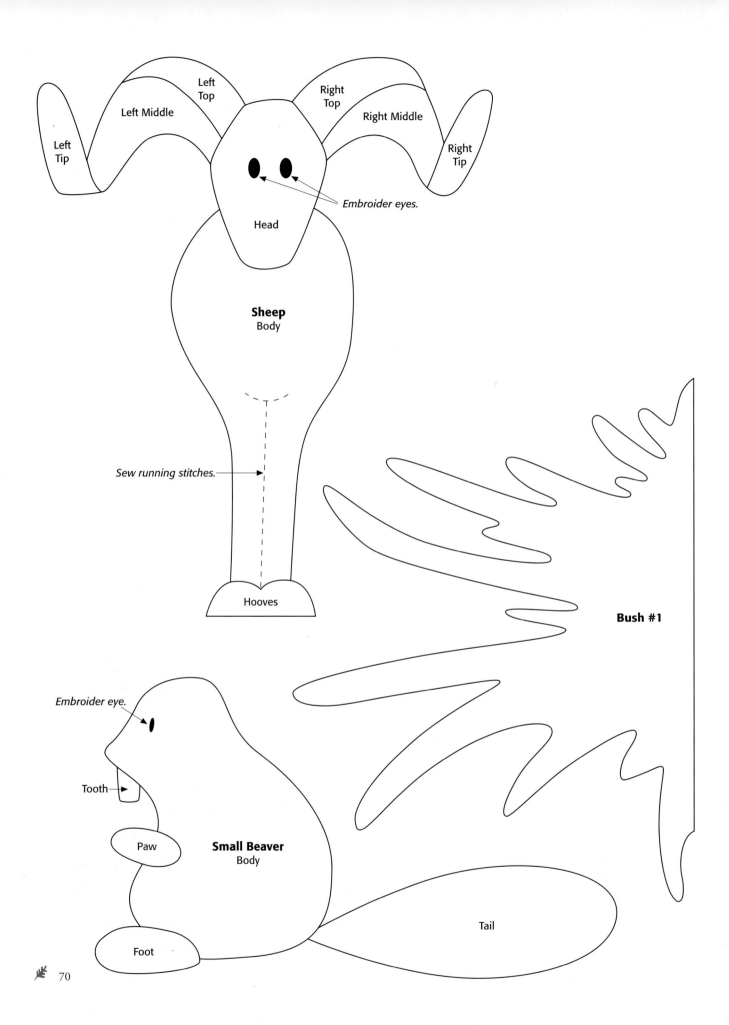

Left Tip

Left Middle

Left Top

Right Top

Right Middle

Right Tip

Embroider eyes.

Head

Sheep
Body

Sew running stitches.

Hooves

Bush #1

Embroider eye.

Tooth

Paw

Small Beaver
Body

Tail

Foot

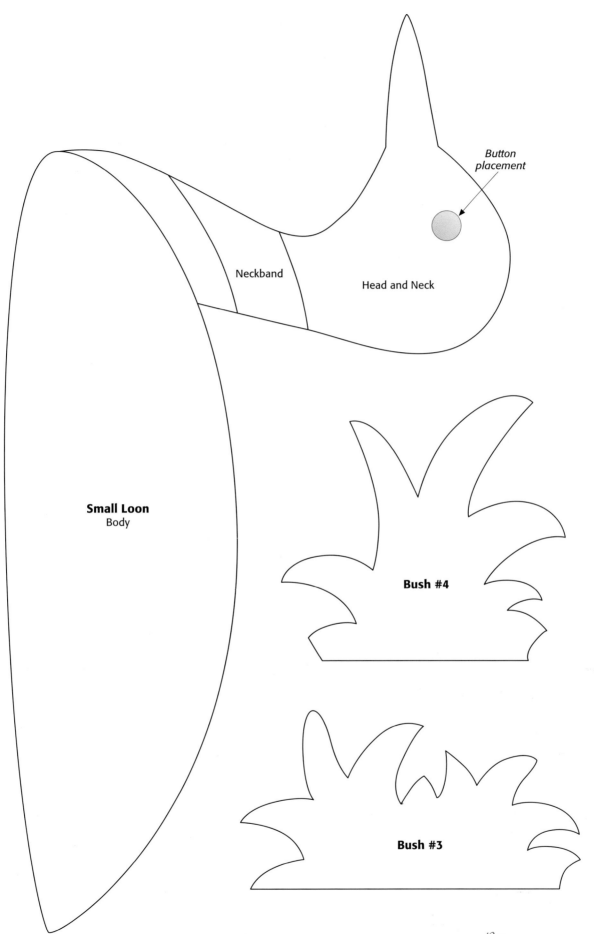

Button
placement

Neckband

Head and Neck

Small Loon
Body

Bush #4

Bush #3

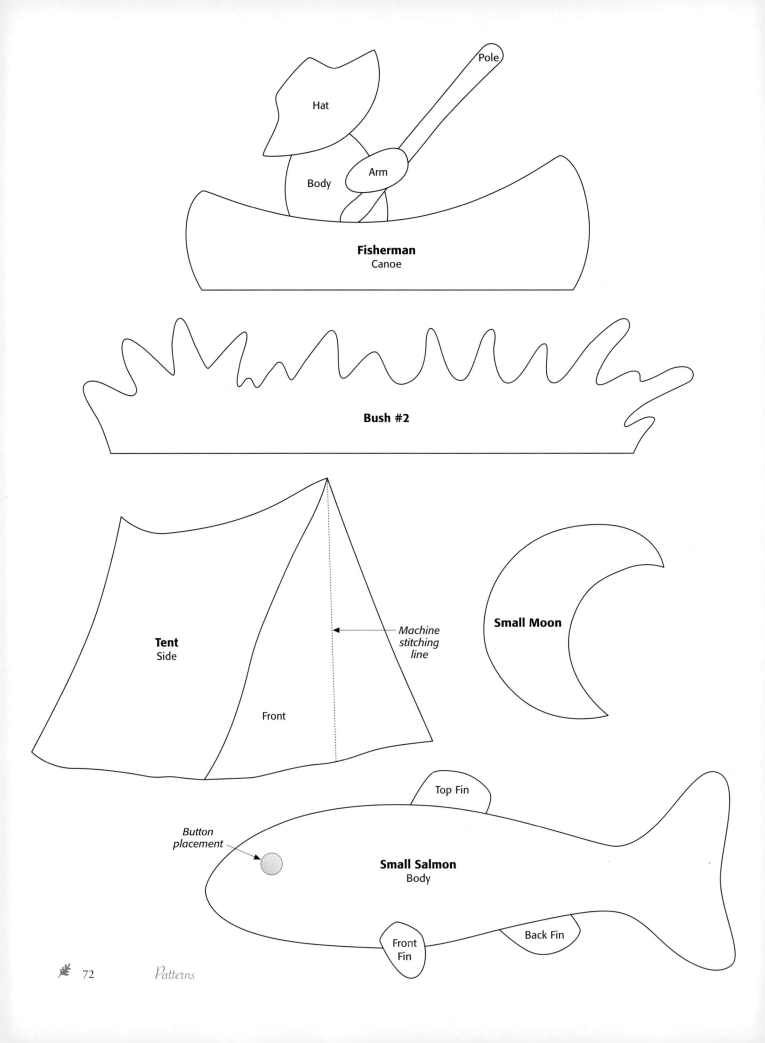

Pole

Hat

Body

Arm

Fisherman
Canoe

Bush #2

Tent
Side

Front

← *Machine stitching line*

Small Moon

Button placement

Top Fin

Small Salmon
Body

Front Fin

Back Fin

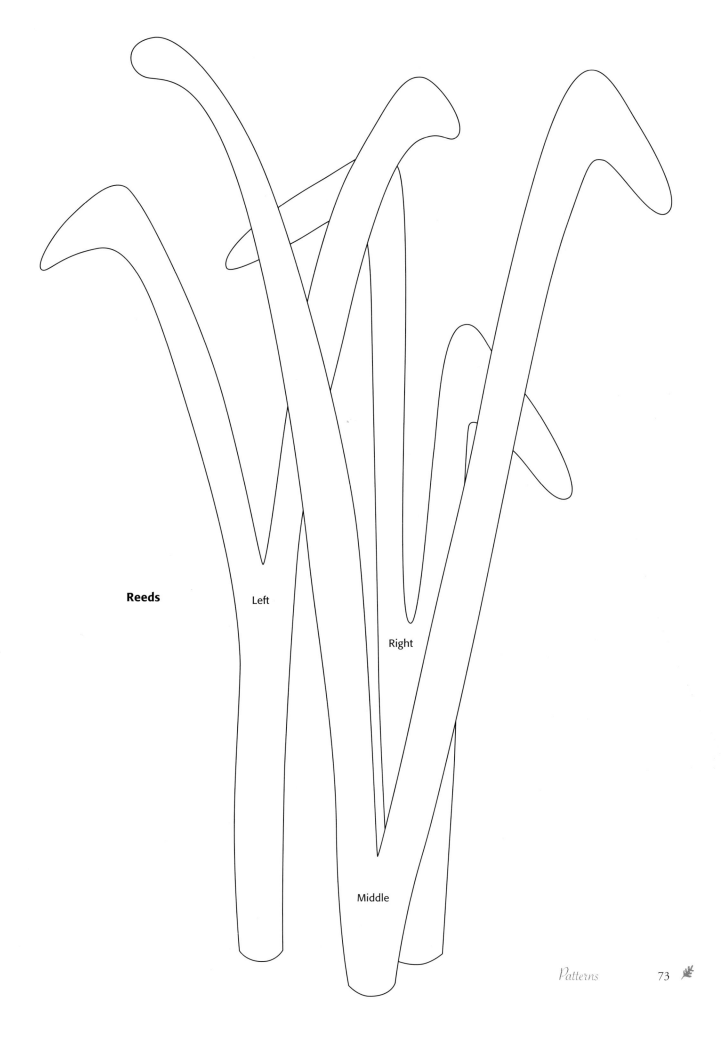

Reeds

Left

Right

Middle

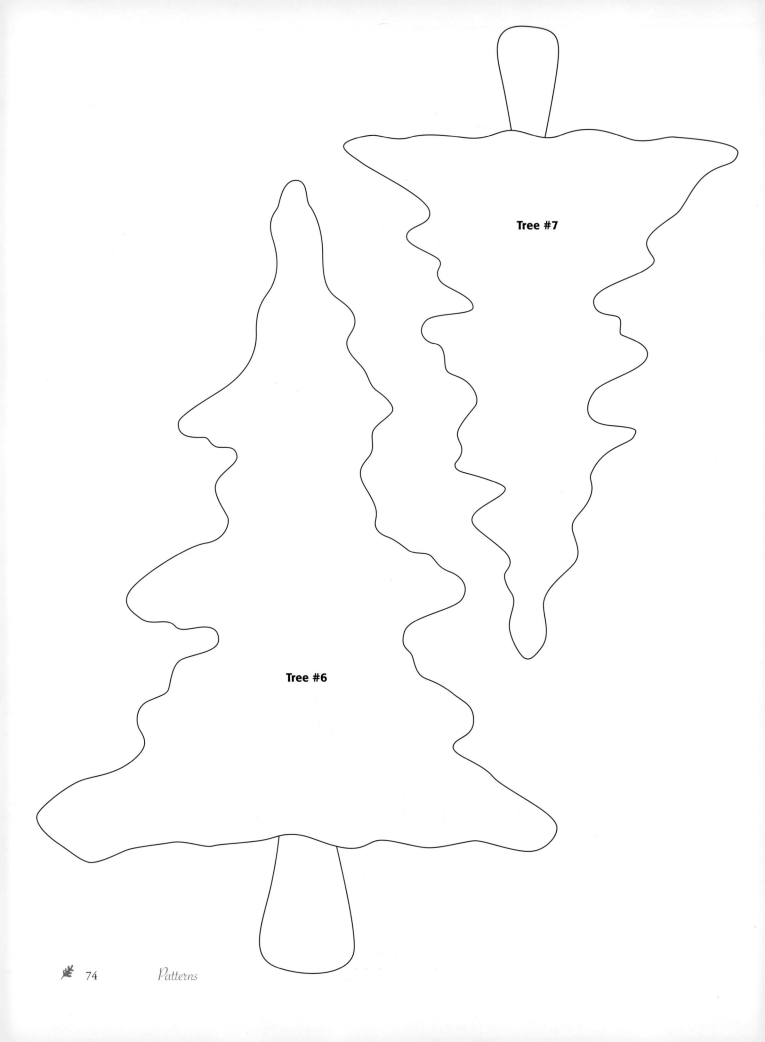

Tree #7

Tree #6

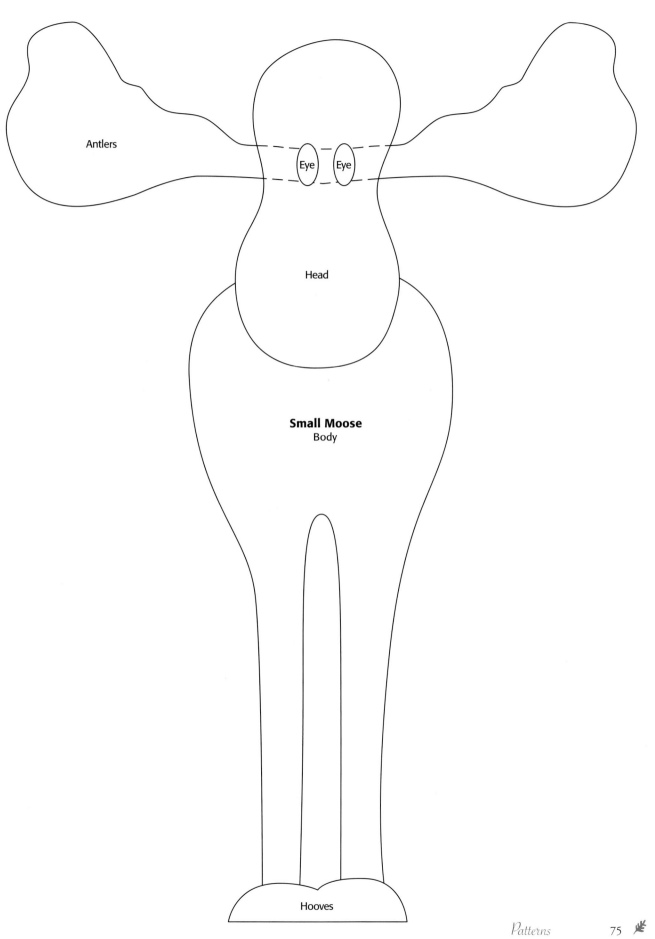

Antlers

Eye Eye

Head

Small Moose
Body

Hooves

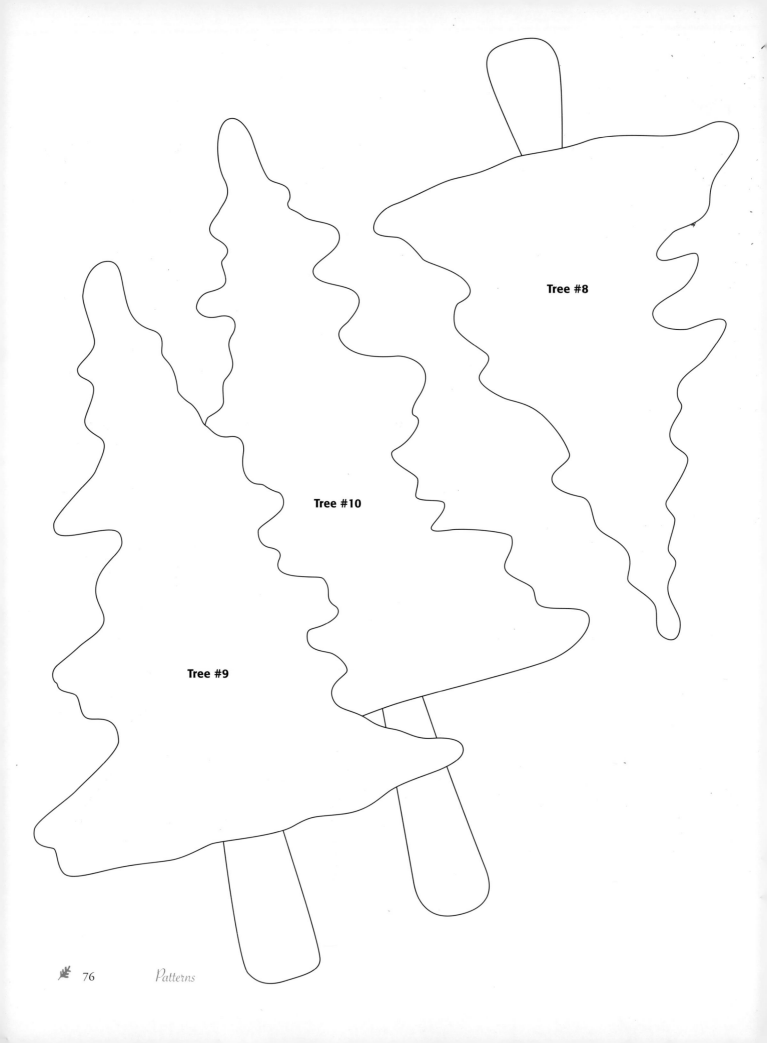

Tree #8

Tree #10

Tree #9

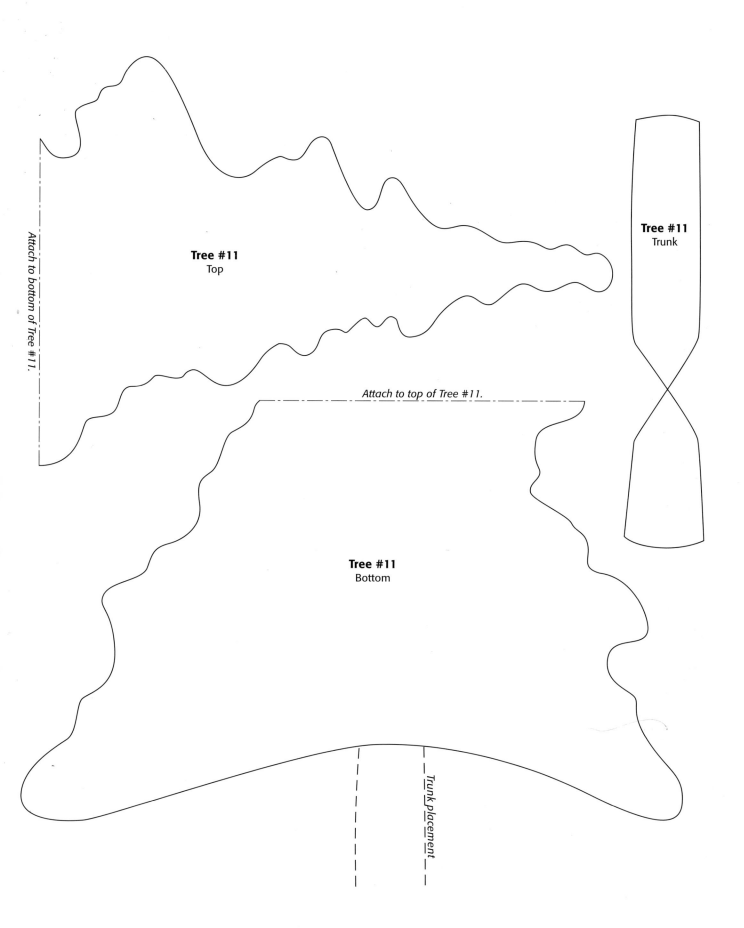

Attach to bottom of Tree #11.

Tree #11
Top

Tree #11
Trunk

Attach to top of Tree #11.

Tree #11
Bottom

Trunk placement

¼" seam allowance

Cabin
Background
Cut 1 and 1 reversed.

Straight of grain

Place on fold.

Cabin
Roof
Cut 1.

About the Authors

CORI DERKSEN

My husband, Randy; daughter, Kierra; and I enjoy living on acreage west of Winkler, Manitoba. Our property borders a creek and twenty acres of densely treed land that is filled with all sorts of wildlife: deer, beaver, rabbits, and fox, just to name a few. As you can see, the projects in this book are a reflection of our lifestyle and our surroundings. What better way to combine my love of quilts with the beauty of nature!

MYRA HARDER

I live in Winkler, Manitoba, with my husband, Mark, and our son, Samson. I love our great outdoors, and I try to reflect that style in our home and in the projects that I make. We live in an area where each season is distinct and the outdoors gives you something new to enjoy with each change in the weather. While Mark has outdoor hobbies that cover every season, I find that the Canadian winters provide the perfect time to plan and piece quilt tops.

We have been friends for twenty-two years and working together has become quite natural. Instead of the sandbox and swing set, we now play with fabrics and quilts.

In January 2001, our first book, *Down in the Valley: Paper Pieced Houses and Buildings,* was released. Our designs have also appeared in *American Patchwork and Quilting* in 1999 and 2000. Since our first book was released, we have begun teaching projects out of our book and are enjoying our new playground! This has been an exciting adventure, and we look forward to many more new and wonderful quilting experiences.

new and bestselling titles from

Martingale™
& C O M P A N Y
America's Best-Loved Craft & Hobby Books™

That Patchwork Place®
America's Best-Loved Quilt Books®

NEW RELEASES
Artful Album Quilts
Biblical Blocks
Christmas at That Patchwork Place™
Color Moves
Colorwash Bargello Quilts
Country Threads
Creating Quilts with Simple Shapes
Creating with Paint
The Decorated Porch
Easy Paper-Pieced Baby Quilts
Flannel Quilts
For the Birds
In the Studio with Judy Murrah
Instant Fabric
More Quick Watercolor Quilts
Paper Piece a Flower Garden
Patchwork Picnic
Scrap Frenzy

APPLIQUÉ
Artful Appliqué
Colonial Appliqué
Red and Green: An Appliqué Tradition
Rose Sampler Supreme
Your Family Heritage: Projects in Appliqué

BABY QUILTS
The Quilted Nursery
Quilts for Baby: Easy as ABC
More Quilts for Baby: Easy as ABC
Even More Quilts for Baby: Easy as ABC

HOLIDAY QUILTS
Easy and Fun Christmas Quilts
Paper Piece a Merry Christmas
A Snowman's Family Album Quilt
Welcome to the North Pole

LEARNING TO QUILT
Basic Quiltmaking Techniques for:
    Borders and Bindings
    Curved Piecing
    Divided Circles
    Eight-Pointed Stars
    Hand Appliqué
    Machine Appliqué
    Strip Piecing
The Joy of Quilting
The Quilter's Handbook
Your First Quilt Book (or it should be!)

PAPER PIECING
50 Fabulous Paper-Pieced Stars
A Quilter's Ark
Easy Machine Paper Piecing
Needles and Notions
Paper-Pieced Curves
Show Me How to Paper Piece

ROTARY CUTTING
101 Fabulous Rotary-Cut Quilts
365 Quilt Blocks a Year Perpetual Calendar
Fat Quarter Quilts
Lap Quilting Lives!
Quick Watercolor Quilts
Quilts from Aunt Amy
Spectacular Scraps
Time-Crunch Quilts

SMALL & MINIATURE QUILTS
Celebrate! with Little Quilts
Easy Paper-Pieced Miniatures
Little Quilts All Through the House

CRAFTS
300 Papermaking Recipes
The Art of Handmade Paper
   and Collage
The Art of Stenciling
Creepy Crafty Halloween
Gorgeous Paper Gifts
Grow Your Own Paper
Instant Fabric
Stamp with Style
Wedding Ribbonry

KNITTING
Comforts of Home
Fair Isle Sweaters Simplified
Knit It Your Way
Knitted Shawls, Stoles, and Scarves
Knitting with Novelty Yarns
Paintbox Knits
Simply Beautiful Sweaters
Simply Beautiful Sweaters for Men
Two Sticks and a String
The Ultimate Knitter's Guide
Welcome Home: Kaffe Fassett

Our books are available at bookstores and your favorite craft, fabric and yarn retailers. If you don't see the title you're looking for, visit us at www.martingale-pub.com or contact us at:

1-800-426-3126

International: 1-425-483-3313

Fax: 1-425-486-7596

E-mail: info@martingale-pub.com

For more information and a full list of our titles, visit our Web site or call for a free catalog.
